COLLECTED WORKS
OF
EDGAR A. GUEST

COLLECTED WORKS
OF
EDGAR A. GUEST

Making the House a Home and
When Day is Done

BIBLIOBAZAAR

COLLECTED WORKS
OF
EDGAR A. GUEST

CONTENTS

MAKING THE HOUSE A HOME

Here's our story, page by page,
Happy youth and middle-age,
Smile and tear-drop, weal and woe
Such as all who live must know—
Here it is all written down,
Not for glory or renown,
But the hope when we are gone
Those who bravely follow on
Meeting care and pain and grief
Will not falter in belief.

MAKING THE HOUSE A HOME

We have been building a home for the last fifteen years, but it begins to look now as though it will not be finished for many years to come. This is not because the contractors are slow, or the materials scarce, or because we keep changing our minds. Rather it is because it takes years to build a home, whereas a house can be builded in a few months.

Mother and I started this home-building job on June 28th, 1906. I was twenty-five years of age; and she—well, it is sufficient for the purposes of this record to say that she was a few years younger. I was just closing my career as police reporter for the Detroit "Free Press," when we were married. Up to a few months before our wedding, my hours had been from three o'clock, in the afternoon, until three o'clock in the morning, every day of the week except Friday. Those are not fit hours for a married man—especially a young married man. So it was fortunate for me that my managing editor thought I might have possibilities as a special writer, and relieved me from night duty.

It was then we began to plan the home we should build. It was to be a hall of contentment and the abiding place of joy and beauty. And it was all going to be done on the splendid salary of twenty-eight dollars a week. That sum doesn't sound like much now, but to us, in January, 1906, it was independence. The foundation of our first home was something less than five hundred dollars, out of which was also to come the extravagance of a two-weeks' honeymoon trip.

Fortunately for all of us, life does not break its sad news in advance. Dreams are free, and in their flights of fancy young folks may be as extravagant as they wish. There may be breakers ahead, and trials, days of discouragement and despair, but life tells us nothing of them to spoil our dreaming.

We knew the sort of home we wanted, but we were willing to begin humbly. This was not because we were averse to starting at the top. Both Mother and I had then, and have now, a fondness for the best things of life. We should have liked a grand piano, and a self-making ice box, and a servant, and an automobile right off! But less than five hundred dollars capital and twenty-eight dollars a week salary do not provide those things.

What we *could* have would be a comfortable flat, and some nice furniture. We'd pay cash for all we could, and buy the remainder of the necessary things on time. We had found a wonderful, brand-new flat which we could rent for twenty-five dollars a month. It had hardwood floors, steam heat, two big bedrooms, a fine living room with a gas grate, a hot-water heater for the bath, and everything modern and convenient. Today the landlord would ask ninety dollars a month for that place and tell you he was losing money at that.

With the rent paid, we should have eighty-seven dollars a month left to live on. The grocery bill, at that time, would not run more than twenty dollars a month; telephone, gas, and electric light would not exceed ten dollars a month; the milkman and the paper boy would take but little, and in winter time a ton of coal per month would be sufficient. Oh, we should have plenty of money, and could easily afford to pledge twenty dollars a month to pay for necessary furniture.

It will be noticed that into our dreaming came no physician, no dentist, no expenses bobbing up from unexpected sources. Not a single bill collector called at the front door of our dream castle to ask for money which we did not have.

If older and wiser heads suggested the possibility of danger, we produced our plans on paper, and asked them from whence could trouble come? Today we understand the depth of the kindly smile which our protests always evoked. They were letting the dreamers dream.

At last the furniture was bought on the installment plan and the new flat was being put in order. It called for a few more pieces of furniture than we had figured on, and the debt, in consequence, was greater; but that meant merely a few months more to make payments.

It was fine furniture, too! Of course it has long since ceased to serve us; but never in this world shall that dining set be duplicated! For perfection of finish and loveliness of design, that first oak dining table will linger in our memories for life. The one we now have cost more than all the money we spent for all the furniture with which we began housekeeping; and yet, figuring according to the joy it has brought to us, it is poor in comparison.

And so it was, too, with the mahogany settee, upholstered in green plush, and the beveled glass dresser, and the living-room chairs. We used to make evening trips over to that flat merely for the joy of admiring these things—our things; the first we had ever possessed.

Then came the night of June 27th. We had both looked forward to that wonderful honeymoon trip up the lakes to Mackinac Island, and tomorrow we were to start. But right then I am sure that both Mother and I wished we might call it off. It seemed so foolish to go away from such a beautiful flat and such lovely furniture.

The honeymoon trip lasted two weeks; and one day, at Mackinac Island, I found Mother in tears.

"What the matter?" I asked.

"I want to go home!" she said. "I know I am silly and foolish, but I want to get back to our own house and our own furniture, and arrange our wedding presents, and hang the curtains, and put that set of Haviland china in the cabinet!"

So back we came to begin our home-building in earnest.

The rent and the furniture installments came due regularly, just as we had expected. So did the gas and electric light and telephone bills. But, somehow or other, our dream figures and the actual realities did not balance. There never was a month when there was as much left of our eighty-seven dollars as we had figured there should have been.

For one thing, I was taken ill. That brought the doctor into the house; and since then we have always had him to reckon with and to settle with. Then there was an insurance policy to keep up. In our dream days, the possibility of my dying sometime had never entered our heads; but now it was an awful reality. And that quarterly premium developed a distressing habit of falling due at the most inopportune times. Just when we thought we should have at least twenty dollars for ourselves, in would come the little yellow slip informing us that the thirty days' grace expired on the fifth.

But the home-of-our-own was still in our dreams. We were happy, but we were going to be still happier. If ever we could get rid of those furniture installments we could start saving for the kind of home we wanted.

Then, one evening, Mother whispered the happiest message a wife ever tells a husband. We were no longer to live merely for ourselves; there was to be another soon, who should bind us closer together and fill our lives with gladness.

But—and many a night we sat for hours and planned and talked and wondered—*how* were we to meet the expense? There was nothing in the savings bank, and much was needed there. Mother had cherished for years her ideas for her baby's outfit. They would cost money; and I would be no miserly father, either! My child should have the best of everything, somehow. It was up to me to get it, somehow, to . . . If only that furniture were paid for!

Then a curious event occurred. I owed little bills amounting to about twenty-one dollars. This sum included the gas, electric light, and telephone bills, on which an added sum was charged if unpaid before the tenth of the month. I had no money to meet them. I was worried and discouraged. To borrow that sum would have been easy, but to pay it back would have been difficult.

That very morning, into the office came the press agent of a local theatre, accompanied by Mr. Henry Dixey, the well-known actor. Mr. Dixey wanted two lyrics for songs. He had the ideas which he wished expressed in rhyme, and wondered whether or not I would attempt them. I promised him that I would, and on the spot he handed me twenty-five dollars in cash to bind the bargain. If those songs proved successful I should have more.

The way out had been provided! From Mr. Dixey's point of view, those songs were not a success; but from mine they were, for they bridged me over a chasm I had thought I could not leap. I never heard from that pair of songs afterward; but neither Mother nor I will ever forget the day they were written.

It meant more than the mere paying of bills, too. It taught us to have faith—faith in ourselves and faith in the future. There is always a way out of the difficulties. Even though we cannot see or guess what that way is to be, it will be provided. Since then we have gone together through many dark days and cruel hurts and bitter disappointments, but always to come out stronger for the test.

The next few months were devoted to preparations for the baby, and our financial reckonings had to be readjusted. I had to find ways of making a little more money. I was not after much money, but I must have more. All I had to sell was what I could write. Where was a quick market for a poor newspaper man's wares?

My experience with Mr. Dixey turned me to the vaudeville stage. I could write playlets, I thought. So while Mother was busy sewing at nights I devoted myself to writing. And at last the first sketch was finished. At the Temple Theatre that week was the popular character actor, William H. Thompson. To him I showed the manuscript of the sketch, which was called "The Matchmaker." Mr. Thompson took it on Tuesday; and on Friday he sent word that he wished to see me. Into his dressing-room I went, almost afraid to face him.

"It's a bully little sketch," said he, as I sat on his trunk, "and I'd like to buy it from you. I can't pay as much as I should like; but if you care to let me have it I'll give you two hundred and fifty dollars—one hundred and fifty dollars now, and the remaining hundred next week."

I tried to appear indifferent, but the heart of me was almost bursting with excitement. It meant that the furniture bill was as good as paid! And there would be money in the bank for the first time since we were married! The deal was made, and I left the theatre with the largest sum of money I had ever made all at once. Later someone said to me that I was foolish to sell that sketch outright for so little money.

"Foolish!" said I. "That two hundred and fifty dollars looked bigger to me than the promise of a thousand some day in the future!"

Once more the way out had been provided.

And then came the baby—a glorious little girl—and the home had begun to be worth-while. There was a new charm to the walls and halls. The oak table and the green plush settee took on a new glory.

I was the usual proud father, with added variations of my own. One of my pet illusions was that none, save Mother and me, was to be trusted to hold our little one. When others *would* take her, I stood guard to catch her if in some careless moment they should let her fall.

As she grew older, my collars became finger-marked where her little hands had touched them. We had pictures on our walls, of course, and trinkets on the mantelpiece, and a large glass mirror which had been one of our wedding gifts. These things had become commonplace to us—until the baby began to notice them! Night after night, I would take her in my arms and show her the sheep in one of the pictures, and talk to her about them, and she would coo delightedly. The trinkets on the mantelpiece became dearer to us because she loved to handle them. The home was being sanctified by her presence. We had come into a new realm of happiness.

But a home cannot be builded always on happiness. We were to learn that through bitter experience. We had seen white crepe on other doors, without ever thinking that some day it might flutter on our own. We had witnessed sorrow, but had never suffered it. Our home had welcomed many a gay and smiling visitor; but there was a grim and sinister one to come, against whom no door can be barred.

After thirteen months of perfect happiness, its planning and dreaming, the baby was taken from us.

The blow fell without warning. I left home that morning, with Mother and the baby waving their usual farewells to me from the window. Early that afternoon, contrary to my usual custom, I decided to go home in advance of my regular time. I had no reason for doing this, aside from a strange unwillingness to continue at work. I recalled later that I cleaned up my desk and put away a number of things, as though I were going away for some time. I never before had done that, and nothing had occurred which might make me think I should not be back at my desk as usual.

When I reached home the baby was suffering from a slight fever, and Mother already had called the doctor in. He diagnosed it as only a slight disturbance. During dinner, I thought baby's breathing was not as regular as it should be, and I summoned the doctor immediately. Her condition grew rapidly worse, and a second physician was called; but it was not in human skill to save her. At eleven o'clock that night she was taken from us.

It is needless to dwell here upon the agony of that first dark time through which we passed. That such a blow could leave loveliness in its path, and add a touch of beauty to our dwelling place, seemed unbelievable at the time. Yet today our first baby still lives with us, as wonderful as she was in those glad thirteen months. She has not grown older, as have we, but smiles that same sweet baby smile of hers upon us as of old. We can talk of her now bravely and proudly; and we have come to understand that it was a privilege to have had her, even for those brief thirteen months.

To have joys in common is the dream of man and wife. We had supposed that love was based on mutual *happiness*. And Mother and I had been happy together; we had been walking arm in arm under blue skies, and we knew how much we meant to each other. But just how much we *needed* each other neither of us really knew—until we had to share a common sorrow.

To be partners in a sacred memory is a divine bond. To be partners in a little mound, in one of God's silent gardens, is the closest relationship which man and woman can know on this earth. Our lives had been happy before; now they had been made beautiful.

So it was with the home. It began to mean more to us, as we began each to mean more to the other. The bedroom in which our baby fell asleep seemed glorified. Of course there were the lonely days and weeks and months when everything we touched or saw brought back the memory of her. I came home many an evening to find on Mother's face the mark of tears; and I knew she had been living over by herself the sorrow of it all.

I learned how much braver the woman has to be than the man. I could go into town, where there was the contagion of good cheer; and where my work absorbed my thoughts and helped to shut out grief. But not so with Mother! She must live day by day and hour by hour amid the scenes of her anguish. No matter where she turned, something reminded her of the joy we had known and lost. Even the striking clock called back to her mind the hour when something should have been done for the baby.

"I *must* have another little girl," she sobbed night after night. "I *must* have another little girl!"

And once more the way out was provided. We heard of a little girl who was to be put out for adoption; she was of good but unfortunate parents. We proposed to adopt her.

I have heard many arguments against adopting children, but I have never heard a good one. Even the infant doomed to die could enrich, if only for a few weeks, the lives of a childless couple, and they would be happier for the rest of their days in the knowledge that they had tried to do something worthy in this world and had made comfortable the brief life of a little one.

"What if the child should turn out wrong?" I hear often from the lips of men and women.

"What of that?" I reply. "You can at least be happy in the thought that you have tried to do something for another."

To childless couples everywhere I would say with all the force I can employ, *adopt a baby*! If you would make glorious the home you are building; if you would fill its rooms with laughter and contentment; if you would make your house more than a place in which to eat and sleep; if you would fill it with happy memories and come yourselves into a closer and more perfect union, adopt a baby! Then, in a year or two, adopt another. He who spends money on a little child is investing it to real purpose; and the dividends it pays in pride and happiness and contentment are beyond computation.

Marjorie came to us when she was three years old. She bubbled over with mirth and laughter and soothed the ache in our hearts. She filled the little niches and corners of our lives with her sweetness, and became not only ours in name, but ours also in love and its actualities.

There were those who suggested that we were too young to adopt a child. They told us that the other children would undoubtedly be sent to us as time went on. I have neither the space here nor the inclination to list the imaginary difficulties outlined to us as the possibilities of adoption.

But Mother and I talked it all over one evening. And we decided that we needed Marjorie, and Marjorie needed us. As to the financial side of the question, I smiled.

"I never heard of anyone going to the poorhouse, or into bankruptcy," I said, "because of the money spent on a child. I fancy I can pay the bills."

That settled it. The next evening when I came home, down the stairway leading to our flat came the cry, "Hello, Daddy!" from one of the sweetest little faces I have ever seen. And from that day, until God needed her more and called her home, that "Hello, Daddy" greeted me and made every care worth while.

The little home had begun to grow in beauty once more. That first shopping tour for Marjorie stands out as an epoch in our lives. I am not of the right sex to describe it. Marjorie came to us with only such clothing as a poor mother could provide. She must be outfitted anew from head to toe, and she was. The next evening, when she greeted me, she was the proud possessor of more lovely things than she had ever known before. But, beautiful as the little face appeared to me then, more beautiful was the look in Mother's face. There had come into her eyes a look of happiness which had been absent for many months. I learned then, and I state it now as a positive fact, that a woman's greatest happiness comes from dressing a little girl. Mothers may like pretty clothes for themselves; but to put pretty things on a little girl is an infinitely greater pleasure. More than once Mother went down-town for something for herself—only to return without it, but with something for Marjorie!

We pledged to ourselves at the very beginning that we would make Marjorie ours; not only to ourselves but to others. Our friends were asked never to refer in her presence to the fact that she was adopted. As far as we were concerned it was dismissed from our minds. She was three years old when she was born to us, and from then on we were her father and her mother. To many who knew her and loved her, this article will be the first intimation they ever have received that Marjorie was not our own flesh and blood. It was her pride and boast that she was like her mother, but had her father's eyes. Both her mother and I have smiled hundreds of times, as people meeting her for the first time would say, "Anyone would know she belonged to you. She looks exactly like you!"

Marjorie made a difference in our way of living. A second-story flat, comfortable though it was, was not a good place to bring up a little girl. More than ever, we needed a home of our own. But to need and to provide are two different propositions. We needed a back yard; but

24

back yards are expensive; and though newspapermen may make good husbands they seldom make "good money."

One evening Mother announced to me that she had seen the house we ought to have. It had just been completed, had everything in it her heart had wished for, and could be bought for forty-two hundred dollars. The price was just forty-two hundred dollars more than I had!

All I did have was the wish to own a home of my own. But four years of our married life had gone, and I was no nearer the first payment on a house than when we began as man and wife. However, I investigated and found that I could get this particular house by paying five hundred dollars down and agreeing to pay thirty-five a month on the balance. I could swing thirty-five a month, but the five hundred was a high barrier.

Then I made my first wise business move. I went to Julius Haass, president of the Wayne County and Home Savings Bank, who always had been my friend, and explained to him my difficulties. He loaned me that five hundred dollars for the first payment—I to pay it back twenty-five dollars monthly—and the house was ours.

We had become land owners overnight. My income had increased, of course; but so had my liabilities. The first few years of that new house taxed our ingenuity more than once. We spent now and then, not money which we had, but money which we were *going to get*; but it was buying happiness. If ever a couple have found real happiness in this world we found it under the roof of that Leicester Court home.

There nearly all that has brought joy and peace and contentment into our lives was born to us. It was from there I began to progress; it was there my publishers found me; and it was there little Bud was born to us. We are out of it now. We left it for a big reason; but we drive by it often just to see it; for it is still ours in the precious memory of the years we spent within its walls.

Still, in the beginning, it was just a house! It had no associations and no history. It had been built to sell. The people who paid for its construction saw in its growing walls and rooftree only the few hundred dollars they hoped to gain. It was left to us to change that *house* into a *home*. It sounds preachy, I know, to say that all buildings depend for their real beauty upon the spirit of the people who inhabit them. But it is true.

As the weeks and months slipped by, the new house began to soften and mellow under Mother's gentle touches. The living-room assumed an air of comfort; my books now had a real corner of their own; the guest-chamber—or, rather, the little spare-room—already had entertained its transient tenants; and as our friends came and went the walls caught something from them all, to remind us of their presence.

I took to gardening. The grounds were small, but they were large enough to teach me the joy of an intimate friendship with growing things. Today, in my somewhat larger garden, I have more than one hundred and fifty rosebushes, and twenty or thirty peony clumps, and I know their names and their habits. The garden has become a part of the home. It is not yet the garden I dream of, nor even the garden which I think it will be next year; but it is the place where play divides the ground with beauty. What Bud doesn't require for a baseball diamond the roses possess.

Early one morning in July, Bud came to us. Immediately, the character of that front bedroom was changed. It was no longer just "our bedroom;" it was "the room where Bud was born." Of all the rooms in all the houses of all the world, there is none so gloriously treasured in the memories of man and woman as those wherein their children have come to birth.

I have had many fine things happen to me: Friends have borne me high on kindly shoulders; out of the depths of their generous hearts they have given me honors which I have not deserved; I have more than once come home proud in the possession of some new joy, or of some task accomplished; but I have never known, and never shall know, a thrill of happiness to equal that which followed good old Doctor Gordon's brief announcement: "It's a Boy!"

"It's a Boy!" All that day and the next I fairly shouted it to friends and strangers. To Marjorie's sweetness, and to the radiant loveliness of the little baby which was ours for so brief a time, had been added the strength and roguishness of a boy.

The next five years saw the walls of our home change in character. Finger marks and hammer marks began to appear. When Bud had reached the stage where he could walk, calamity began to follow in his trail. Once he tugged at a table cover and the open bottle of ink fell upon the rug. There was a great splotch of ink forever to be visible to all who entered that living-room! Yet even that black stain became in time a part of us. We grew even to boast of it. We pointed it out to new acquaintances as the place where Bud spilled the ink. It was an evidence of his health and his natural tendencies. It proved to all the world that in Bud we had a real boy; an honest-to-goodness boy who could spill ink—and *would*, if you didn't keep a close watch on him.

Then came the toy period of our development. The once tidy house became a place where angels would have feared to tread in the dark. Building blocks and trains of cars and fire engines and a rocking horse were everywhere, to trip the feet of the unwary. Mother scolded about it, at times; and I fear I myself have muttered harsh things when, late at night, I have entered the house only to stumble against the tin sides of an express wagon.

But I have come to see that toys in a house are its real adornments. There is no pleasanter sight within the front door of any man's castle than the strewn and disordered evidences that children there abide. The house seems unfurnished without them.

This chaos still exists in our house today. Mother says I encourage it. Perhaps I do. I know that I dread the coming day when the home shall become neat and orderly and silent and precise. What is more, I live in horror of the day when I shall have to sit down to a meal and not send a certain little fellow away from the table to wash his hands. That has become a part of the ceremonial of my life. When the evening comes that he will appear for dinner, clean and immaculate, his shirt buttoned properly and his hair nicely brushed, perhaps Mother will be proud of him; but as for me, there will be a lump in my throat—for I shall know that he has grown up.

Financially, we were progressing. We had a little more "to do with," as Mother expressed it; but sorrow and grief and anxiety were not through with us.

We were not to be one hundred per cent happy. No one ever is. Marjorie was stricken with typhoid fever, and for fourteen weeks we fought that battle; saw her sink almost into the very arms of death; and watched her pale and wasted body day by day, until at last the fever broke and she was spared to us.

Another bedroom assumed a new meaning to us both. We knew it as it was in the dark hours of night; we saw the morning sun break through its windows. It was the first room I visited in the morning and the last I went to every night. Coming home, I never stopped in hall or living-room, but hurried straight to her. All there was in that home then was Marjorie's room! We lived our lives within it. And gradually, her strength returned and we were happy again.

But only for a brief time . . . Early the following summer I was called home by Doctor Johnson. When I reached there, he met me at the front door, smiling as though to reassure me.

"You and Bud are going to get out," said he. "Marjorie has scarlet fever."

Bud had already been sent to his aunt Florence's. I was to gather what clothing I should need for six weeks, and depart.

If I had been fond of that home before, I grew fonder of it as the days went by. I think I never knew how much I valued it until I was shut out from it. I could see Mother and Marjorie through the window, but I was not to enter. And I grew hungry for a sight of the walls with their finger marks, and of the ink spot on the rug. We had been six years in the building of that home. Somehow, a part of us had been woven into every nook and corner of it.

But Marjorie was not thriving. Her cheeks were pale and slightly flushed. The removal of tonsils didn't help. Followed a visit to my dentist. Perhaps a tooth was spreading poison through her system. He looked at her, and after a few minutes took me alone into his private office.

"I'm sorry, Eddie," he said. "I am afraid it isn't teeth. You have a long, hard fight to make—if it is what I think it is."

Tuberculosis had entered our home. It had come by way of typhoid and scarlet fevers. The specialist confirmed Doctor Oakman's suspicions, and our battle began. The little home could serve us no longer. It was not the place for such a fight for life as we were to make. Marjorie must have a wide-open sleeping porch; and the house lacked that, nor could one be built upon it.

And so we found our present home. It was for sale at a price I thought then I should never be able to pay. We could have it by making a down payment of seventy-five hundred dollars, the balance to be covered by a mortgage. But I neither had that much, nor owned securities for even a small fraction of it.

But I did have a friend: a rich, but generous friend! I told him what I wanted; and he seemed more grieved at my burden than concerned with my request. He talked only of Marjorie and her chances; he put his arm about my shoulders, and I knew he was with me.

"What do you need?" he asked.

"Seventy-five hundred dollars in cash."

He smiled.

"Have a lawyer examine the abstract to the property, and if it is all right come back to me."

In two days I was back. The title to the house was clear. He smiled again, and handed me his check for the amount, with not a scratch of the paper between us.

I suggested something of that sort to him.

"The important thing is to get the house," he said. "When that is done and you have the deed to it and the papers all fixed up, you come back and we'll fix up our little matter." And that is how it was done.

So into our present home we moved. We had a bigger and a better and a costlier dwelling place. We were climbing upward. But we were also beginning once more with just a house. Just a house—but founded on a mighty purpose! It was to become home to us, even more dearly loved than the one we were leaving.

For four years it has grown in our affections. Hope has been ours. We have lived and laughed and sung and progressed . . . But we have also wept and grieved.

Twice the doctor had said we were to conquer. Then came last spring and the end of hope. Week after week, Marjorie saw the sunbeams filter through the windows of her open porch; near by, a pair of robins built their nest; she watched them and knew them and named them. We planned great things together and great journeys we should make. That they were not to be she never knew . . . And then she fell asleep . . .

Her little life had fulfilled its mission. She had brought joy and beauty and faith into our hearts; she had comforted us in our hours of loneliness and despair; she had been the little cheerful builder of our home—and perhaps God needed her.

She continued to sleep for three days, only for those three days her sun porch was a bower of roses. On Memorial Day, Mother and I stood once more together beside a little mound where God had led us. Late that afternoon we returned to the home to which Marjorie had taken us. It had grown more lovely with the beauty which has been ours, because of her.

* * * * *

The home is not yet completed. We still cherish our dreams of what it is to be. We would change this and that. But, after all, what the home

30

is to be is not within our power to say. We hope to go forward together, building and changing and improving it. Tomorrow shall see something that was not there yesterday. But through sun and shade, through trial and through days of ease and of peace, it is our hope that something of our best shall still remain. Whatever happens, it is our hope that what may be "just a house" to many shall be to us the home we have been building for the last fifteen years.

HOME

It takes a heap o' livin' in a house t' make it home,
A heap o' sun an' shadder, an' ye sometimes have t' roam
Afore ye really 'preciate the things ye lef' behind,
An' hunger fer 'em somehow, with 'em allus on yer mind.
It don't make any differunce how rich ye get t' be,
How much yer chairs an' tables cost, how great yer luxury;
It ain't home t' ye, though it be the palace of a king,
Until somehow yer soul is sort o' wrapped round everything.

Home ain't a place that gold can buy or get up in a minute;
Afore it's home there's got t' be a heap o' livin' in it;
Within the walls there's got t' be some babies born, and then
Right there ye've got t' bring 'em up t' women good, an' men;
And gradjerly, as time goes on, ye find ye wouldn't part
With anything they ever used—they've grown into yer heart:
The old high chairs, the playthings, too, the little shoes they wore

Ye hoard; an' if ye could ye'd keep the thumbmarks on the door.
Ye've got t' weep t' make it home, ye've got t' sit an' sigh
An' watch beside a loved one's bed, an' know that Death is nigh;
An' in the stillness o' the night t' see Death's angel come,
An' close the eyes o' her that smiled, an' leave her sweet voice dumb.

Fer these are scenes that grip the heart, an' when yer tears are dried,
Ye find the home is dearer than it was, an' sanctified;
An' tuggin' at ye always are the pleasant memories
O' her that was an' is no more—ye can't escape from these.

Ye've got t' sing an' dance fer years, ye've got t' romp an' play,
An' learn t' love the things ye have by usin' 'em each day;
Even the roses 'round the porch must blossom year by year
Afore they 'come a part o' ye, suggestin' someone dear
Who used t' love 'em long ago, an' trained 'em jes' t' run
The way they do, so's they would get the early mornin' sun;
Ye've got t' love each brick an' stone from cellar up t' dome:
It takes a heap o' livin' in a house t' make it home.

[*From "A Heap o' Livin"*]

WHEN DAY IS DONE

To
S.H.D.
A real friend who never knows when day is done

WHEN DAY IS DONE

When day is done and the night slips down,
And I've turned my back on the busy town,
And come once more to the welcome gate
Where the roses nod and the children wait,
I tell myself as I see them smile
That life is good and its tasks worth while.

When day is done and I've come once more
To my quiet street and the friendly door,
Where the Mother reigns and the children play
And the kettle sings in the old-time way,
I throw my coat on a near-by chair
And say farewell to my pack of care.

When day is done, all the hurt and strife
And the selfishness and the greed of life,
Are left behind in the busy town;
I've ceased to worry about renown
Or gold or fame, and I'm just a dad,
Content to be with his girl and lad.

Whatever the day has brought of care,
Here love and laughter are mine to share,
Here I can claim what the rich desire—
Rest and peace by a ruddy fire,
The welcome words which the loved ones speak
And the soft caress of a baby's cheek.

When day is done and I reach my gate,
I come to a realm where there is no hate,
For here, whatever my worth may be,
Are those who cling to their faith in me;
And with love on guard at my humble door,
I have all that the world has struggled for.

THE SIMPLE THINGS

I would not be too wise—so very wise
    That I must sneer at simple songs and creeds,
And let the glare of wisdom blind my eyes
    To humble people and their humble needs.

I would not care to climb so high that I
    Could never hear the children at their play,
Could only see the people passing by,
    And never hear the cheering words they say.

I would not know too much—too much to smile
    At trivial errors of the heart and hand,
Nor be too proud to play the friend the while,
    Nor cease to help and know and understand.

I would not care to sit upon a throne,
    Or build my house upon a mountain-top,
Where I must dwell in glory all alone
    And never friend come in or poor man stop.

God grant that I may live upon this earth
    And face the tasks which every morning brings
And never lose the glory and the worth
    Of humble service and the simple things.

LIFE IS WHAT WE MAKE IT

Life is a jest;
   Take the delight of it.
Laughter is best;
   Sing through the night of it.
Swiftly the tear
   And the hurt and the ache of it
Find us down here;
   Life must be what we make of it.

Life is a song;
   Dance to the thrill of it.
Grief's hours are long,
   And cold is the chill of it.
Joy is man's need;
   Let us smile for the sake of it.
This be our creed:
   Life must be what we make of it.

Life is a soul;
   The virtue and vice of it,
Strife for a goal,
   And man's strength is the price of it.
Your life and mine,
   The bare bread and the cake of it
End in this line:
   Life must be what we make of it.

WHAT WE NEED

We were settin' there an' smokin' of our pipes, discussin' things,
Like licker, votes for wimmin, an' the totterin'thrones o' kings,
When he ups an' strokes his whiskers with his hand an' says t'me:
"Changin' laws an' legislatures ain't, as fur as I can see,
Goin' to make this world much better, unless somehow we can
Find a way to make a better an' a finer sort o' man.

"The trouble ain't with statutes or with systems—not at all;
It's with humans jest like we air an' their petty ways an' small.
We could stop our writin' law-books an' our regulatin' rules
If a better sort of manhood was the product of our schools.
For the things that we air needin' ain't no writin' from a pen
Or bigger guns to shoot with, but a bigger typeof men.

"I reckon all these problems air jest ornery like the weeds.
They grow in soil that oughta nourish only decent deeds,
An' they waste our time an' fret us when, if we were thinkin' straight
An' livin' right, they wouldn't be so terrible an' great.
A good horse needs no snaffle, an' a good man, I opine,
Doesn't need a law to check him or to force him into line.

"If we ever start in teachin' to our children, year by year,
How to live with one another, there'll be less o' trouble here.
If we'd teach 'em how to neighbor an' to walk in honor's ways,
We could settle every problem which the mind o' man can raise.
What we're needin' isn't systems or some regulatin' plan,
But a bigger an' a finer an' a truer type o' man."

A BOY AND HIS DAD

A boy and his dad on a fishing-trip—
There is a glorious fellowship!
Father and son and the open sky
And the white clouds lazily drifting by,
And the laughing stream as it runs along
With the clicking reel like a martial song,
And the father teaching the youngster gay
How to land a fish in the sportsman's way.

I fancy I hear them talking there
In an open boat, and the speech is fair;
And the boy is learning the ways of men
From the finest man in his youthful ken.
Kings, to the youngster, cannot compare
With the gentle father who's with him there.
And the greatest mind of the human race
Not for one minute could take his place.

Which is happier, man or boy?
The soul of the father is steeped in joy,
For he's finding out, to his heart's delight,
That his son is fit for the future fight.

He is learning the glorious depths of him,
And the thoughts he thinks and his every whim,
And he shall discover, when night comes on,
How close he has grown to his little son.

A boy and his dad on a fishing-trip—
Oh, I envy them, as I see them there
Under the sky in the open air,
For out of the old, old long-ago
Come the summer days that I used to know,
When I learned life's truths from my father's lips
As I shared the joy of his fishing-trips—
Builders of life's companionship!

IF I HAD YOUTH

If I had youth I'd bid the world to try me;
    I'd answer every challenge to my will.
And though the silent mountains should defy me,
    I'd try to make them subject to my skill.
I'd keep my dreams and follow where they led me;
    I'd glory in the hazards which abound.
I'd eat the simple fare privations fed me,
    And gladly make my couch upon the ground.

If I had youth I'd ask no odds of distance,
    Nor wish to tread the known and level ways.
I'd want to meet and master strong resistance,
    And in a worth-while struggle spend my days.
I'd seek the task which calls for full endeavor;
    I'd feel the thrill of battle in my veins.
I'd bear my burden gallantly, and never
    Desert the hills to walk on common plains.

If I had youth no thought of failure lurking
    Beyond tomorrow's dawn should fright my soul.
Let failure strike—it still should find me working
    With faith that I should some day reach my goal.

I'd dice with danger—aye!—and glory in it;
    I'd make high stakes the purpose of my throw.
I'd risk for much, and should I fail to win it,
    I would not ever whimper at the blow.

If I had youth no chains of fear should bind me;
    I'd brave the heights which older men must shun.
I'd leave the well-worn lanes of life behind me,
    And seek to do what men have never done.
Rich prizes wait for those who do not waver;
    The world needs men to battle for the truth.
It calls each hour for stronger hearts and braver.
    This is the age for those who still have youth!

LOOKING BACK

I might have been rich if I'd wanted the gold instead of the friendships
 I've made.
I might have had fame if I'd sought for renown in the hours when I
 purposely played.
Now I'm standing today on the far edge of life, and I'm just looking
 backward to see
What I've done with the years and the days that were mine, and all that
 has happened to me.

I haven't built much of a fortune to leave to those who shall carry my
 name,
And nothing I've done shall entitle me now to a place on the tablets of
 fame.
But I've loved the great sky and its spaces of blue; I've lived with the
 birds and the trees;
I've turned from the splendor of silver and gold to share in such pleasures
 as these.

I've given my time to the children who came; together we've romped and
 we've played,
And I wouldn't exchange the glad hours spent with them for the money
 that I might have made.

I chose to be known and be loved by the few, and was deaf to the plaudits of men;
And I'd make the same choice should the chance come to me to live my life over again.

I've lived with my friends and I've shared in their joys, known sorrow with all of its tears;
I have harvested much from my acres of life, though some say I've squandered my years.
For much that is fine has been mine to enjoy, and I think I have lived to my best,
And I have no regret, as I'm nearing the end, for the gold that I might have possessed.

GOD MADE THIS DAY FOR ME

Jes' the sort o' weather and jes' the sort of sky
Which seem to suit my fancy, with the white clouds driftin' by
On a sea o' smooth blue water. Oh, I ain't an egotist,
With an "I" in all my thinkin', but I'm willin' to insist
That the Lord who made us humans an' the birds in every tree
Knows my special sort o' weather an' he made this day fer me.

This is jes' my style o' weather—sunshine floodin' all the place,
An' the breezes from the eastward blowin' gently on my face;
An' the woods chock full o' singin' till you'd think birds never had
A single care to fret 'em or a grief to make 'em sad.
Oh, I settle down contented in the shadow of a tree,
An' tell myself right proudly that the day was made fer me.

It's my day, my sky an' sunshine, an' the temper o' the breeze—
Here's the weather I would fashion could I run things as I please:
Beauty dancin' all around me, music ringin' everywhere,
Like a weddin' celebration—why, I've plumb fergot my care
An' the tasks I should be doin' fer the rainy days to be,
While I'm huggin' the delusion that God made this day fer me.

THE GRATE FIRE

I'm sorry for a fellow if he cannot look and see
In a grate fire's friendly flaming all the joys which used to be.
If in quiet contemplation of a cheerful ruddy blaze
He sees nothing there recalling all his happy yesterdays,
Then his mind is dead to fancy and his life is bleak and bare,
And he's doomed to walk the highways that are always thick with care.

When the logs are dry as tinder and they crackle with the heat,
And the sparks, like merry children, come a-dancing round my feet,
In the cold, long nights of autumn I can sit before the blaze
And watch a panorama born of all my yesterdays.
I can leave the present burdens and the moment's bit of woe,
And claim once more the gladness of the bygone long-ago.

No loved ones ever vanish from the grate fire's merry throng;
No hands in death are folded and no lips are stilled to song.
All the friends who were are living—like the sparks that fly about
They come romping out to greet me with the same old merry shout,
Till it seems to me I'm playing once again on boyhood's stage,
Where there's no such thing as sorrow and there's no such thing as age.

I can be the care-free schoolboy! I can play the lover, too!
I can walk through Maytime orchards with the old sweetheart I knew,
I can dream the glad dreams over, greet the old familiar friends
In a land where there's no parting and the laughter never ends.
All the gladness life has given from a grate fire I reclaim,
And I'm sorry for the fellow-who sees nothing there but flame.

THE HOMELY MAN

Looks as though a cyclone hit him—
Can't buy clothes that seem to fit him;
An' his cheeks are rough like leather,
Made for standin' any weather.
Outwards he was fashioned plainly,
Loose o' joint an' blamed ungainly,
But I'd give a lot if I'd
Been built half as fine inside.

Best thing I can tell you of him
Is the way the children love him.
Now an' then I get to thinkin'
He's much like old Abe Lincoln;
Homely like a gargoyle graven—
Worse'n that when he's unshaven;
But I'd take his ugly phiz
Jes' to have a heart like his.

I ain't over-sentimental,
But old Blake is so blamed gentle
An' so thoughtfull-like of others
He reminds us of our mothers.

Rough roads he is always smoothing
An' his way is, Oh, so soothin',
That he takes away the sting
When your heart is sorrowing.

Children gather round about him
Like they can't get on without him.
An' the old depend upon him,
Pilin' all their burdens on him,
Like as though the thing that grieves 'em
Has been lifted when he leaves 'em.
Homely? That can't be denied,
But he's glorious inside.

THE JOYS WE MISS

There never comes a lonely day but that we miss the laughing ways
Of those who used to walk with us through all our happy yesterdays.
We seldom miss the earthly great—the famous men that life has
known—
But, as the years go racing by, we miss the friends we used to own.

The chair wherein he used to sit recalls the kindly father true
For, Oh, so filled with fun he was, and, Oh, so very much he knew!
And as we face the problems grave with which the years of life are
filled.
We miss the hand which guided us and miss the voice forever stilled.

We little guessed how much he did to smooth our pathway day by day,
How much of joy he brought to us, how much of care he brushed
away;
But now that we must tread alone the thorough-fare of life, we find
How many burdens we were spared by him who was so brave and kind.

Death robs the living, not the dead—they sweetly sleep whose tasks are
done;
But we are weaker than before who still must live and labor on.
For when come care and grief to us, and heavy burdens bring us woe,
We miss the smiling, helpful friends on whom we leaned long years ago.

We miss the happy, tender ways of those who brought us mirth and
  cheer;
We never gather round the hearth but that we wish our friends were
  near;
For peace is born of simple things—a kindly word, a goodnight kiss,
The prattle of a babe, and love—these are the vanished joys we miss.

THE FELLOWSHIP OF BOOKS

I care not who the man may be,
  Nor how his tasks may fret him,
Nor where he fares, nor how his cares
  And troubles may beset him,
If books have won the love of him,
  Whatever fortune hands him,
He'll always own, when he's alone,
  A friend who understands him.

Though other friends may come and go,
  And some may stoop to treason,
His books remain, through loss or gain,
  And season after season
The faithful friends for every mood,
  His joy and sorrow sharing,
For old time's sake, they'll lighter make
  The burdens he is bearing.

Oh, he has counsel at his side,
  And wisdom for his duty,
And laughter gay for hours of play,
  And tenderness and beauty,
And fellowship divinely rare,
  True friends who never doubt him,
Unchanging love, and God above,
  Who keeps good books about him.

WHEN SORROW COMES

When sorrow comes, as come it must,
In God a man must place his trust.
There is no power in mortal speech
The anguish of his soul to reach,
No voice, however sweet and low,
Can comfort him or ease the blow.

He cannot from his fellowmen
Take strength that will sustain him then.
With all that kindly hands will do,
And all that love may offer, too,
He must believe throughout the test
That God has willed it for the best.

We who would be his friends are dumb;
Words from our lips but feebly come;
We feel, as we extend our hands,
That one Power only understands
And truly knows the reason why
So beautiful a soul must die.

We realize how helpless then
Are all the gifts of mortal men.
No words which we have power to say
Can take the sting of grief away—
That Power which marks the sparrow's fall
Must comfort and sustain us all.

When sorrow comes, as come it must,
In God a man must place his trust.
With all the wealth which he may own,
He cannot meet the test alone,
And only he may stand serene
Who has a faith on which to lean.

GOLF LUCK

As a golfer I'm not one who cops the money;
    I shall always be a member of the dubs;
There are times my style is positively funny;
    I am awkward in my handling of the clubs.
I am not a skillful golfer, nor a plucky,
    But this about myself I proudly say—
When I win a hole by freaky stroke or lucky,
    I never claim I played the shot that way.

There are times, despite my blundering behavior,
    When fortune seems to follow at my heels;
Now and then I play supremely in her favor,
    And she lets me pull the rankest sort of steals;
She'll give to me the friendliest assistance,
    I'll jump a ditch at times when I should not,
I'll top the ball and get a lot of distance—
    But I don't claim that's how I played the shot.

I've hooked a ball when just that hook I needed,
    And wondered how I ever turned the trick;
I've thanked my luck for what a friendly tree did,
    Although my fortune made my rival sick;

Sometimes my shots turn out just as I planned 'em,
   The sort of shots I usually play,
But when up to the cup I chance to land 'em,
   I never claim I played 'em just that way.

There's little in my game that will commend me;
   I'm not a shark who shoots the course in par;
I need good fortune often to befriend me;
   I have my faults and know just what they are.
I play golf in a desperate do-or-die way,
   And into traps and trouble oft I stray,
But when by chance the breaks are coming my way,
   I do not claim I played the shots that way.

CONTRADICTIN' JOE

Heard of Contradictin' Joe?
Most contrary man I know.
Always sayin', "That's not so."

Nothing's ever said, but he
Steps right up to disagree—
Quarrelsome as he can be.

If you start in to recite
All the details of a fight,
He'll butt in to set you right.

Start a story that is true,
He'll begin correctin' you—
Make you out a liar, too!

Mention time o' year or day,
Makes no difference what you say,
Nothing happened just that way.

Bet you, when his soul takes flight,
An' the angels talk at night,
He'll butt in to set 'em right.

There where none should have complaints
He will be with "no's" and "ain'ts"
Contradictin' all the saints.

THE BETTER JOB

If I were running a factory
I'd stick up a sign for all to see;
I'd print it large and I'd nail it high
On every wall that the men walked by;
And I'd have it carry this sentence clear:
"The 'better job' that you want is here!"

It's the common trait of the human race
To pack up and roam from place to place;
Men have done it for ages and do it now;
Seeking to better themselves somehow
They quit their posts and their tools they drop
For a better job in another shop.

It may be I'm wrong, but I hold to this—
That something surely must be amiss
When a man worth while must move away
For the better job with the better pay;
And something is false in our own renown
When men can think of a better town.

So if I were running a factory
I'd stick up this sign for all to see,
Which never an eye in the place could miss:
"There isn't a better town than this!
You need not go wandering, far or near—
The 'better job' that you want is here!"

MY RELIGION

My religion's lovin' God, who made us, one and all,
Who marks, no matter where it be, the humble sparrow's fall;
An' my religion's servin' Him the very best I can
By not despisin' anything He made, especially man!
It's lovin' sky an' earth an' sun an' birds an' flowers an' trees,
But lovin' human beings more than any one of these.

I ain't no hand at preachin' an' I can't expound the creeds;
I fancy every fellow's faith must satisfy his needs
Or he would hunt for something else. An' I can't tell the why
An' wherefore of the doctrines deep—and what's more I don't try.
I reckon when this life is done and we can know His plan,
God won't be hard on anyone who's tried to be a man.

My religion doesn't hinge on some one rite or word;
I hold that any honest prayer a mortal makes is heard;
To love a church is well enough, but some get cold with pride
An' quite forget their fellowmen for whom the Saviour died;
I fancy he best worships God, when all is said an' done,
Who tries to be, from day to day, a friend to everyone.

If God can mark the sparrow's fall, I don't believe He'll fail
To notice us an' how we act when doubts an' fears assail;
I think He'll hold what's in our hearts above what's in our creeds,
An' judge all our religion here by our recorded deeds;
An' since man is God's greatest work since life on earth began,
He'll get to Heaven, I believe, who helps his fellowman.

WHAT I CALL LIVING

The miser thinks he's living when he's hoarding up his gold;
The soldier calls it living when he's doing something bold;
The sailor thinks it living to be tossed upon the sea,
And upon this vital subject no two of us agree.
But I hold to the opinion, as I walk my way along,
That living's made of laughter and good-fellowship and song.

I wouldn't call it living always to be seeking gold,
To bank all the present gladness for the days when I'll be old.
I wouldn't call it living to spend all my strength for fame,
And forego the many pleasures which today are mine to claim.
I wouldn't for the splendor of the world set out to roam,
And forsake my laughing children and the peace I know at home.
Oh, the thing that I call living isn't gold or fame at all!

It's good-fellowship and sunshine, and it's roses by the wall;
It's evenings glad with music and a hearth fire that's ablaze,
And the joys which come to mortals in a thousand different ways.
It is laughter and contentment and the struggle for a goal;
It is everything that's needful in the shaping of a soul.

IF THIS WERE ALL

If this were all of life we'll know,
    If this brief space of breath
Were all there is to human toil,
    If death were really death,
And never should the soul arise
    A finer world to see,
How foolish would our struggles seem,
    How grim the earth would be!

If living were the whole of life,
    To end in seventy years,
How pitiful its joys would seem!
    How idle all its tears!
There'd be no faith to keep us true,
    No hope to keep us strong,
And only fools would cherish dreams—
    No smile would last for long.

How purposeless the strife would be
    If there were nothing more,
If there were not a plan to serve,
    An end to struggle for!
No reason for a mortal's birth
    Except to have him die—
How silly all the goals would seem
    For which men bravely try.

There must be something after death;
    Behind the toil of man
There must exist a God divine
    Who's working out a plan;
And this brief journey that we know
    As life must really be
The gateway to a finer world
    That some day we shall see.

A CHRISTMAS CAROL

God bless you all this Christmas Day
And drive the cares and griefs away.
Oh, may the shining Bethlehem star
Which led the wise men from afar
Upon your heads, good sirs, still glow
To light the path that ye should go.

As God once blessed the stable grim
And made it radiant for Him;
As it was fit to shield His Son,
May thy roof be a holy one;
May all who come this house to share
Rest sweetly in His gracious care.

Within thy walls may peace abide,
The peace for which the Savior died.
Though humble be the rafters here,
Above them may the stars shine clear,
And in this home thou lovest well
May excellence of spirit dwell.

God bless you all this Christmas Day;
May Bethlehem's star still light thy way
And guide thee to the perfect peace
When every fear and doubt shall cease.
And may thy home such glory know
As did the stable long ago.

FORGOTTEN BOYHOOD

He wears a long and solemn face
And drives the children from his place;
He doesn't like to hear them shout
Or race and run and romp about,
And if they chance to climb his tree,
He is as ugly as can be.
If in his yard they drive a ball,
Which near his pretty flowers should fall,
He hides the leather sphere away,
Thus hoping to prevent their play.

The youngsters worry him a lot,
This sorry man who has forgot
That once upon a time, he too
The self-same mischief used to do.
The boyhood he has left behind
Has strangely vanished from his mind,
And he is old and gray and cross
For having suffered such a loss.
He thinks he never had the joy
That is the birthright of a boy.

He has forgotten how he ran,
Or to a dog's tail tied a can,
Broke window panes, and loved to swipe
Some neighbor's apples, red and ripe—
He thinks that always, day or night,
His conduct was exactly right.
In boys today he cannot see
The youngster that he used to be,
Forgotten is that by-gone day,
When he was mischievous as they.

Poor man! I'm sorry for your lot.
The best of life you have forgot.
Could you remember what you were,
Unharnessed and untouched by spur,
These youngsters that you drive away
Would be your comrades here today.
Among them you could gayly walk
And share their laughter and their talk;
You could be young and blithe as they,
Could you recall your yesterday.

THE PEAKS OF VALOR

These are the peaks of valor; keeping clean your father's name,
Too brave for petty profit to risk the brand of shame,
Adventuring for the future, yet mindful of the past,
For God, for country and for home, still valorous to the last.

These are the peaks of valor: a speech that knows no lie,
A standard of what's right and wrong which no man's wealth can buy,
All unafraid of failure, to venture forth to fight,
Yet never for the victory's sake to turn away from right.

Ten thousand times the victor is he who fails to win,
Who could have worn the conqueror's crown by stooping low in sin;
Ten thousand times the braver is he who turns away
And scorns to crush a weaker man that he may rule the day.

These are the peaks of valor: standing firm and standing true
To the best your father taught you and the best you've learned anew,
Helpful to all who need you, winning what joys you can,
Writing in triumph to the end your record as a man.

WHEN THE MINISTER CALLS

My Paw says that it used to be,
Whenever the minister came for tea,
'At they sat up straight in their chairs at night
An' put all their common things out o' sight,
An' nobody cracked a joke or grinned,
But they talked o' the way that people sinned,
An' the burnin' fires that would cook you sure
When you came to die, if you wasn't pure—
Such a gloomy affair it used to be
Whenever the minister came for tea.

But now when the minister comes to call
I get him out for a game of ball,
And you'd never know if you'd see him bat,
Without any coat or vest or hat,
That he is a minister, no, siree!
He looks like a regular man to me.
An' he knows just how to go down to the dirt
For the grounders hot without gettin' hurt—
An' when they call us, both him an' me
Have to git washed up again for tea.

Our minister says if you'll just play fair
You'll be fit for heaven or anywhere;
An' fun's all right if your hands are clean
An' you never cheat an' you don't get mean.
He says that he never has understood
Why a feller can't play an' still be good.
An' my Paw says that he's just the kind
Of a minister that he likes to find—
So I'm always tickled as I can be
Whenever our minister comes for tea.

THE AGE OF INK

Swiftly the changes come. Each day
Sees some lost beauty blown away
And some new touch of lovely grace
Come into life to take its place.
The little babe that once we had
One morning woke a roguish lad;
The babe that we had put to bed
Out of our arms and lives had fled.

Frocks vanished from our castle then,
Ne'er to be worn or seen again,
And in his knickerbocker pride
He boasted pockets at each side
And stored them deep with various things—
Stones, tops and jacks and-colored strings;
Then for a time we claimed the joy
Of calling him our little boy.

Brief was the reign of such a spell.
One morning sounded out a bell;
With tears I saw her brown eyes swim
And knew that it was calling him.
Time, the harsh master of us all,
Was bidding him to heed his call;
This shadow fell across life's pool—
Our boy was on his way to school.

Our little boy! And still we dreamed,
For such a little boy he seemed!
And yesterday, with eyes aglow
Like one who has just come to know
Some great and unexpected bliss,
He bounded in, announcing this:
"Oh, Dad! Oh, Ma! Say, what d'you think?
This year we're going to write with ink!"

Here was a change I'd not foreseen,
Another step from what had been.
I paused a little while to think
About this older age of ink—
What follows this great step, thought I,
What next shall come as the time goes by?
And something said: "His pathway leads
Unto the day he'll write with deeds."

NO USE SIGHIN'

No use frettin' when the rain comes down,
No use grievin' when the gray clouds frown,
No use sighin' when the wind blows strong,
No use wailin' when the world's all wrong;
Only thing that a man can do
Is work an' wait till the sky gets blue.

No use mopin' when you lose the game,
No use sobbin' if you're free from shame,
No use cryin' when the harm is done,
Just keep on tryin' an' workin' on;
Only thing for a man to do,
Is take the loss an' begin anew.

No use weepin' when the milk is spilled,
No use growlin' when your hopes are killed,
No use kickin' when the lightnin' strikes
Or the floods come along an' wreck your dykes;
Only thing for a man right then
Is to grit his teeth an' start again.

For it's how life is an' the way things are
That you've got to face if you travel far;
An' the storms will come an' the failures, too,
An' plans go wrong spite of all you do;
An' the only thing that will help you win,
Is the grit of a man and a stern set chin.

NO CHILDREN!

No children in the house to play—
It must be hard to live that way!
I wonder what the people do
When night comes on and the work is through,
With no glad little folks to shout,
No eager feet to race about,
No youthful tongues to chatter on
About the joy that's been and gone?
The house might be a castle fine,
But what a lonely place to dine!

No children in the house at all,
No fingermarks upon the wall,
No corner where the toys are piled—
Sure indication of a child.
No little lips to breathe the prayer
That God shall keep you in His care,
No glad caress and welcome sweet
When night returns you to your street;
No little lips a kiss to give—
Oh, what a lonely way to live!

No children in the house! I fear
We could not stand it half a year.
What would we talk about at night,
Plan for and work with all our might,
Hold common dreams about and find
True union of heart and mind,
If we two had no greater care
Than what we both should eat and wear?
We never knew love's brightest flame
Until the day the baby came.

And now we could not get along
Without their laughter and their song.
Joy is not bottled on a shelf,
It cannot feed upon itself,
And even love, if it shall wear,
Must find its happiness in care;
Dull we'd become of mind and speech
Had we no little ones to teach.
No children in the house to play!
Oh, we could never live that way!

THE LOSS IS NOT SO GREAT

It is better as it is: I have failed but I can sleep;
Though the pit I now am in is very dark and deep
I can walk tomorrow's streets and can meet tomorrow's men
Unashamed to face their gaze as I go to work again.

I have lost the hope I had; in the dust are all my dreams,
But my loss is not so great or so dreadful as it seems;
I made my fight and though I failed I need not slink away
For I do not have to fear what another man may say.

They may call me over-bold, they may say that I was frail;
They may tell I dared too much and was doomed at last to fail;
They may talk my battle o'er and discuss it as they choose,
But I did no brother wrong—I'm the only one to lose.

It is better as it is: I have kept my self-respect.
I can walk tomorrow's streets meeting all men head erect.
No man can charge his loss to a pledge I did not keep;
I have no shame to regret: I have failed, but I can sleep.

DAN MCGANN DECLARES HIMSELF

Said Dan McGann to a foreign man who worked at the selfsame bench,
"Let me tell you this," and for emphasis he flourished a Stilson wrench;
"Don't talk to me of the bourjoissee, don't open your mouth to speak
Of your socialists or your anarchists, don't mention the bolsheveek,
For I've had enough of this foreign stuff, I'm sick as a man can be
Of the speech of hate, and I'm tellin' you straight that this is the land for
 me!

"If you want to brag, just take that flag an' boast of its field o' blue,
An' praise the dead an' the blood they shed for the peace o' the likes o' you.
Enough you've raved," and once more he waved his wrench in a forceful
 way,
"O' the cunning creed o' some Russian breed; I stand for the U.S.A.!
I'm done with your fads, and your wild-eyed lads. Don't flourish your rag
 o' red
Where I can see or by night there'll be tall candles around your bed.

"So tip your hat to a flag like that! Thank God for its stripes an' stars!
Thank God you're here where the roads are clear, away from your kings
 and czars.
I can't just say what I feel today, for I'm not a talkin' man,
But, first an' last, I am standin' fast for all that's American.
So don't you speak of the bolsheveek, it's sick of that stuff I am!
One God, one flag is the creed I brag! I'm boostin' for Uncle Sam."

A BOY AND HIS STOMACH

What's the matter with you—ain't I always been your friend?
Ain't I been a pardner to you? All my pennies don't I spend
In gettin' nice things for you? Don't I give you lots of cake?
Say, stummick, what's the matter, that you had to go an' ache?

Why, I loaded you with good things yesterday, I gave you more
Potatoes, squash an' turkey than you'd ever had before.
I gave you nuts an' candy, pumpkin pie an' chocolate cake,
An' las' night when I got to bed you had to go an' ache.

Say, what's the matter with you—ain't you satisfied at all?
I gave you all you wanted, you was hard jes' like a ball,
An' you couldn't hold another bit of puddin', yet las' night
You ached mos' awful, stummick; that ain't treatin' me jes' right.

I've been a friend to you, I have, why ain't you a friend o' mine?
They gave me castor oil last night because you made me whine.
I'm awful sick this mornin' an' I'm feelin' mighty blue,
'Cause you don't appreciate the things I do for you.

HOME AND THE OFFICE

Home is the place where the laughter should ring,
   And man should be found at his best.
Let the cares of the day be as great as they may,
   The night has been fashioned for rest.
So leave at the door when the toiling is o'er
   All the burdens of worktime behind,
And just be a dad to your girl or your lad—
   A dad of the rollicking kind.

The office is made for the tasks you must face;
   It is built for the work you must do;
You may sit there and sigh as your cares pile up high,
   And no one may criticize you;
You may worry and fret as you think of your debt,
   You may grumble when plans go astray,
But when it comes night, and you shut your desk tight,
   Don't carry the burdens away.

Keep daytime for toil and the nighttime for play,
   Work as hard as you choose in the town,
But when the day ends, and the darkness descends,
   Just forget that you're wearing a frown—
Go home with a smile! Oh, you'll find it worth while;
   Go home light of heart and of mind;
Go home and be glad that you're loved as a dad,
   A dad of the fun-loving kind.

HE'S TAKEN OUT HIS PAPERS

He's taken out his papers, an' he's just like you an' me.
He's sworn to love the Stars and Stripes an' die for it, says he.
An' he's done with dukes an' princes, an' he's done with kings an' queens,
An' he's pledged himself to freedom, for he knows what freedom means.

He's bought himself a bit of ground, an', Lord, he's proud an' glad!
For in the land he came from that is what he never had.
Now his kids can beat his writin', an' they're readin' books, says he,
That the children in his country never get a chance to see.

He's taken out his papers, an' he's prouder than a king:
"It means a lot to me," says he, "just like the breath o' spring,
For a new life lies before us; we've got hope an' faith an' cheer;
We can face the future bravely, an' our kids don't need to fear."

He's taken out his papers, an' his step is light today,
For a load is off his shoulders an' he treads an easier way;
An' he'll tell you, if you ask him, so that you can understand,
Just what freedom means to people who have known some other land.

CASTOR OIL

I don't mind lickin's, now an' then,
An' I can even stand it when
My mother calls me in from play
To run some errand right away.
There's things 'bout bein' just a boy
That ain't all happiness an' joy,
But I suppose I've got to stand
My share o' trouble in this land,
An' I ain't kickin' much—but, say,
The worst of parents is that they
Don't realize just how they spoil
A feller's life with castor oil.

Of all the awful stuff, Gee Whiz!
That is the very worst there is.
An' every time if I complain,
Or say I've got a little pain,
There's nothing else that they can think
'Cept castor oil for me to drink.
I notice, though, when Pa is ill,
That he gets fixed up with a pill,
An' Pa don't handle Mother rough
An' make her swallow nasty stuff;
But when I've got a little ache,
It's castor oil I've got to take.

I don't mind goin' up to bed
Afore I get the chapter read;
I don't mind being scolded, too,
For lots of things I didn't do;
But, Gee! I hate it when they say,
"Come! Swallow this—an' right away!"
Let poets sing about the joy
It is to be a little boy,
I'll tell the truth about my case:
The poets here can have my place,
An' I will take their life of-toil
If they will take my castor oil.

A FATHER'S WISH

What do I want my boy to be?
Oft is the question asked of me,
And oft I ask it of myself—
What corner, niche or post or shelf
In the great hall of life would I
Select for him to occupy?
Statesman or writer, poet, sage
Or toiler for a weekly wage,
Artist or artisan? Oh, what
Is to become his future lot?
For him I do not dare to plan;
I only hope he'll be a man.

I leave it free for him to choose
The tools of life which he shall use,
Brush, pen or chisel, lathe or wrench,
The desk of commerce or the bench,
And pray that when he makes his choice
In each day's task he shall rejoice.
I know somewhere there is a need
For him to labor and succeed;
Somewhere, if he be clean and true,
Loyal and honest through and through,
He shall be fit for any clan,
And so I hope he'll be a man.

I would not build my hope or ask
That he shall do some certain task,
Or bend his will to suit my own;
He shall select his post alone.
Life needs a thousand kinds of men,
Toilers and masters of the pen,
Doctors, mechanics, sturdy hands
To do the work which it commands,
And wheresoe'er he's pleased to go,
Honor and triumph he may know.
Therefore I must do all I can
To teach my boy to be a man.

NO BETTER LAND THAN THIS

If I knew a better country in this glorious world today
Where a man's work hours are shorter and he's drawing bigger pay,
If the Briton or the Frenchman had an easier life than mine,
I'd pack my goods this minute and I'd sail across the brine.
But I notice when an alien wants a land of hope and cheer,
And a future for his children, he comes out and settles here.

Here's the glorious land of Freedom! Here's the milk and honey goal
For the peasant out of Russia, for the long-subjected Pole.
It is here the sons of Italy and men of Austria turn
For the comfort of their bodies and the wages they can earn.
And with all that men complain of, and with all that goes amiss,
There's no happier, better nation on the world's broad face than this.

So I'm thinking when I listen to the wails of discontent,
And some foreign disbeliever spreads his evil sentiment,
That the breed of hate and envy that is sowing sin and shame
In this glorious land of Freedom should go back from whence it came.
And I hold it is the duty, rich or poor, of every man
Who enjoys this country's bounty to be all American.

A BOY AND HIS DOG

A boy and his dog make a glorious pair:
No better friendship is found anywhere,
For they talk and they walk and they run and they play,
And they have their deep secrets for many a day;
And that boy has a comrade who thinks and who feels,
Who walks down the road with a dog at his heels.

He may go where he will and his dog will be there,
May revel in mud and his dog will not care;
Faithful he'll stay for the slightest command
And bark with delight at the touch of his hand;
Oh, he owns a treasure which nobody steals,
Who walks down the road with a dog at his heels.

No other can lure him away from his side;
He's proof against riches and station and pride;
Fine dress does not charm him, and flattery's breath
Is lost on the dog, for he's faithful to death;
He sees the great soul which the body conceals—
Oh, it's great to be young with a dog at your heels!

"WAIT TILL YOUR PA COMES HOME"

"Wait till your Pa comes home!" Oh, dear!
What a dreadful threat for a boy to hear.
Yet never a boy of three or four
But has heard it a thousand times or more.
"Wait till your Pa comes home, my lad,
And see what you'll get for being bad,

"Wait till your Pa comes home, you scamp!
You've soiled the walls with your fingers damp,
You've tracked the floor with your muddy feet
And fought with the boy across the street;
You've torn your clothes and you look a sight!
But wait till your Pa comes home tonight."

Now since I'm the Pa of that daily threat
Which paints me as black as a thing of jet
I rise in protest right here to say
I won't be used in so fierce a way;
No child of mine in the evening gloom
Shall be afraid of my coming home.

I want him waiting for me at night
With eyes that glisten with real delight;
When it's right that punished my boy should be
I don't want the job postponed for me;
I want to come home to a round of joy
And not to frighten a little boy.

"Wait till your Pa comes home!" Oh, dear,
What a dreadful threat for a boy to hear.
Yet that is ever his Mother's way
Of saving herself from a bitter day;
And well she knows in the evening gloam
He won't be hurt when his Pa comes home.

NOTHING TO LAUGH AT

'Taint nothin' to laugh at as I can see!
If you'd been stung by a bumble bee,
An' your nose wuz swelled an' it smarted, too,
You wouldn't want people to laugh at you.
If you had a lump that wuz full of fire,
Like you'd been touched by a red hot wire,
An' your nose spread out like a load of hay,
You wouldn't want strangers who come your way
To ask you to let 'em see the place
An' laugh at you right before your face.

What's funny about it, I'd like to know?
It isn't a joke to be hurted so!
An' how wuz I ever on earth to tell
'At the pretty flower which I stooped to smell
In our backyard wuz the very one
Which a bee wuz busily working on?
An' jus' as I got my nose down there,
He lifted his foot an' kicked for fair,
An' he planted his stinger right into me,
But it's nothin' to laugh at as I can see.

I let out a yell an' my Maw came out
To see what the trouble wuz all about.
She says from my shriek she wuz sure 'at I
Had been struck by a motor car passin' by;
But when she found what the matter wuz
She laughed just like ever'body does
An' she made me stand while she poked about
To pull his turrible stinger out.
An' my Pa laughed, too, when he looked at me,
But it's nothin' to laugh at, as I can see.

My Maw put witch hazel on the spot
To take down the swellin' but it has not.
It seems to git bigger as time goes by
An' I can't see good out o' this one eye;
An' it hurts clean down to my very toes
Whenever I've got to blow my nose.
An' all I can say is when this gits well
There ain't any flowers I'll stoop to smell.
I'm through disturbin' a bumble bee,
But it's nothin' to laugh at, as I can see.

NO ROOM FOR HATE

We have room for the man with an honest dream,
With his heart on fire and his eyes agleam;
We have room for the man with a purpose true,
Who comes to our shores to start life anew,
But we haven't an inch of space for him
Who comes to plot against life and limb.

We have room for the man who will learn our ways,
Who will stand by our Flag in its troubled days;
We have room for the man who will till the soil,
Who will give his hands to a fair day's toil,
But we haven't an inch of space to spare
For the breeder of hatred and black despair.

We have room for the man who will neighbor here,
Who will keep his hands and his conscience clear;
We have room for the man who'll respect our laws
And pledge himself to our country's cause,
But we haven't an inch of land to give
To the alien breed that will alien live.

Against the vicious we bar the gate!
This is no breeding ground for hate.
This is the land of the brave and free
And such we pray it shall always be.
We have room for men who will love our flag,
But none for the friends of the scarlet rag.

THE BOY AND THE FLAG

I want my boy to love his home,
   His Mother, yes, and me:
I want him, wheresoe'er he'll roam,
   With us in thought to be.
I want him to love what is fine,
   Nor let his standards drag,
But, Oh! I want that boy of mine
   To love his country's flag!

I want him when he older grows
   To love all things of earth;
And Oh! I want him, when he knows,
   To choose the things of worth.
I want him to the heights to climb
   Nor let ambition lag;
But, Oh! I want him all the time
   To love his country's flag.

I want my boy to know the best,
   I want him to be great;
I want him in Life's distant West,
   Prepared for any fate.

I want him to be simple, too,
    Though clever, ne'er to brag,
But, Oh! I want him, through and through,
    To love his country's flag.

I want my boy to be a man,
    And yet, in distant years,
I pray that he'll have eyes that can
    Not quite keep back the tears
When, coming from some foreign shore
    And alien scenes that fag,
Borne on its native breeze, once more
    He sees his country's flag.

TOO BIG A PRICE

"They say my boy is bad," she said to me,
    A tired old woman, thin and very frail.
"They caught him robbing railroad cars, an' he
    Must spend from five to seven years in jail.
His Pa an' I had hoped so much for him.
    He was so pretty as a little boy—"
Her eyes with tears grew very wet an' dim—
    "Now nothing that we've got can give us joy!"

"What is it that you own?" I questioned then.
    "The house we live in," slowly she replied,
"Two other houses worked an' slaved for, when
    The boy was but a youngster at my side,
Some bonds we took the time he went to war;
    I've spent my strength against the want of age—
We've always had some end to struggle for.
    Now shame an' ruin smear the final page.

"His Pa has been a steady-goin' man,
    Worked day an' night an' overtime as well;
He's lived an' dreamed an' sweated to his plan
    To own the house an' profit should we sell;
He never drank nor played much cards at night,
    He's been a worker since our wedding day,
He's lived his life to what he knows is right,
    An' why should son of his now go astray?

"I've rubbed my years away on scrubbing boards,
   Washed floors for women that owned less than we,
An' while they played the ladies an' the lords,
   We smiled an' dreamed of happiness to be."
"And all this time where was the boy?" said I.
   "Out somewhere playin'!"—Like a rifle shot
The thought went home—"My God!" she gave a cry,
   "We paid too big a price for what we got."

ALWAYS SAYING "DON'T!"

Folks are queer as they can be,
Always sayin' "don't" to me;
Don't do this an' don't do that.
Don't annoy or tease the cat,
Don't throw stones, or climb a tree,
Don't play in the road. Oh, Gee!
Seems like when I want to play
"Don't" is all that they can say.

If I start to have some fun,
Someone hollers, "Don't you run!"
If I want to go an' play
Mother says: "Don't go away."
Seems my life is filled clear through
With the things I mustn't do.
All the time I'm shouted at:
"No, no, Sonny, don't do that!"

Don't shout so an' make a noise,
Don't play with those naughty boys,
Don't eat candy, don't eat pie,
Don't you laugh and don't you cry,

Don't stand up and don't you fall,
Don't do anything at all.
Seems to me both night an' day
"Don't" is all that they can say.

When I'm older in my ways
An' have little boys to raise,
Bet I'll let 'em race an' run
An' not always spoil their fun;
I'll not tell 'em all along
Everything they like is wrong,
An' you bet your life I won't
All the time be sayin' "don't."

BOY O' MINE

Boy o' mine, boy o' mine, this is my prayer for you,
This is my dream and my thought and my care for you:
Strong be the spirit which dwells in the breast of you,
Never may folly or shame get the best of you;
You shall be tempted in fancied security,
But make no choice that is stained with impurity.

Boy o' mine, boy o' mine, time shall command of you
Thought from the brain of you, work from the hand of you;
Voices of pleasure shall whisper and call to you,
Luring you far from the hard tasks that fall to you;
Then as you're meeting life's bitterest test of men,
God grant you strength to be true as the best of men.

Boy o' mine, boy o' mine, singing your way along,
Cling to your laughter and cheerfully play along;
Kind to your neighbor be, offer your hand to him,
You shall grow great as your heart shall expand to him;
But when for victory sweet you are fighting there,
Know that your record of life you are writing there.

Boy o' mine, boy o' mine, this is my prayer for you;
Never may shame pen one line of despair for you;
Never may conquest or glory mean all to you;
Cling to your honor whatever shall fall to you;
Rather than victory, rather than fame to you,
Choose to be true and let nothing bring shame to you.

TO A LITTLE GIRL

Oh, little girl with eyes of brown
And smiles that fairly light the town,
I wonder if you really know
Just why it is we love you so,
And why—with all the little girls
With shining eyes and tangled curls
That throng and dance this big world through—
Our hearts have room for only you.

Since other little girls are gay
And laugh and sing and romp in play,
And all are beautiful to see,
Why should you mean so much to me?
And why should Mother, day and night,
Make you her source of all delight,
And always find in your caress
Her greatest sum of happiness?

Oh, there's a reason good for this,
You laughing little bright-eyed miss!
In all this town, with all its girls
With shining eyes and sun-kissed curls,

If we should search it through and through
We'd find not one so fair as you;
And none, however fair of face,
Within our hearts could take your place.

For, one glad day not long ago,
God sent you down to us below,
And said that you were ours to keep,
To guard awake and watch asleep;
And ever since the day you came
No other child has seemed the same;
No other smiles are quite so fair
As those which happily you wear.

We seem to live from day to day
To hear the things you have to say;
And just because God gave us you,
We prize the little things you do.
Though God has filled this world with flowers,
We like you best because you're ours—
In you our greatest joys we know,
And that is why we love you so.

A FELLER'S HAT

It's funny 'bout a feller's hat—
He can't remember where it's at,
Or where he took it off, or when,
The time he's wantin' it again.
He knows just where he leaves his shoes;
His sweater he won't often lose;
An' he can find his rubbers, but
He can't tell where his hat is put.

A feller's hat gets anywhere.
Sometimes he'll find it in a chair,
Or on the sideboard, or maybe
It's in the kitchen, just where he
Gave it a toss beside the sink
When he came in to get a drink,
An' then forgot—but anyhow
He never knows where it is now.

A feller's hat is never where
He thinks it is when he goes there;
It's never any use to look
For it upon a closet hook,
'Cause it is always in some place
It shouldn't be, to his disgrace,
An' he will find it, like as not,
Behind some radiator hot.

A feller's hat can get away
From him most any time of day,
So he can't ever find it when
He wants it to go out again;
It hides in corners dark an' grim
An' seems to want to bother him;
It disappears from sight somehow—
I wish I knew where mine is now.

THE GOOD LITTLE BOY

Once there was a boy who never
Tore his clothes, or hardly ever,
Never made his sister mad,
Never whipped fer bein' bad,
Never scolded by his Ma,
Never frowned at by his Pa,
Always fit fer folks to see,
Always good as good could be.

This good little boy from Heaven,
So I'm told, was only seven,
Yet he never shed real tears
When his mother scrubbed his ears,
An' at times when he was dressed
Fer a party, in his best,
He was careful of his shirt
Not to get it smeared with dirt.

Used to study late at night,
Learnin' how to read an' write;
When he played a baseball game,
Right away he always came
When his mother called him in.
An' he never made a din
But was quiet as a mouse
When they'd comp'ny in the house.

Liked to wash his hands an' face,
Liked to work around the place;
Never, when he'd tired of play,
Left his wagon in the way,
Or his bat an' ball around—
Put 'em where they could be found;
An' that good boy married Ma,
An' today he is my Pa.

GREEN APPLE TIME

Green apple time! an', Oh, the joy
Once more to be a healthy boy,
Casting a longin' greedy eye
At every tree he passes by!
Riskin' the direst consequence
To sneak inside a neighbor's fence
An' shake from many a loaded limb
The fruit that seems so near to him
Gosh! but once more I'd like to be
The boy I was in eighty-three.

Here I am sittin' with my pipe,
Waitin' for apples to get ripe;
Waitin' until the friendly sun
Has bronzed 'em all an' says they're done;
Not darin' any more to climb
An' pick a few afore their time.
No legs to run, no teeth to chew
The way that healthy youngsters do;
Jus' old enough to sit an' wait
An' pick my apple from a plate.

Plate apples ain't to be compared
With those you've ventured for an' dared.
It's winnin' 'em from branches high,

Or nippin' 'em when no one's by,
Or findin' 'em the time you feel
You really need another meal,
Or comin' unexpectedly
Upon a farmer's loaded tree
An' grabbin' all that you can eat,
That goes to make an apple sweet.

Green apple time! Go to it, boy,
An' cram yourself right full o' joy;
Watch for the farmer's dog an' run;
There'll come a time it can't be done.
There'll come a day you can't digest
The fruit you've stuffed into your vest,
Nor climb, but you'll sit down like me
An' watch 'em ripening on the tree,
An' jus' like me you'll have to wait
To pick your apples from a plate.

SHE MOTHERED FIVE

She mothered five!
Night after night she watched a little bed,
Night after night she cooled a fevered head,
Day after day she guarded little feet,
Taught little minds the dangers of the street,
Taught little lips to utter simple prayers,
Whispered of strength that some day would be theirs,
And trained them all to use it as they should.
She gave her babies to the nation's good.

She mothered five!
She gave her beauty—from her cheeks let fade
Their rose-blush beauty—to her mother trade.
She saw the wrinkles furrowing her brow,
Yet smiling said: "My boy grows stronger now."
When pleasures called she turned away and said:
"I dare not leave my babies to be fed
By strangers' hands; besides they are too small;
I must be near to hear them when they call."

She mothered five!
Night after night they sat about her knee
And heard her tell of what some day would be.
From her they learned that in the world outside
Are cruelty and vice and selfishness and pride;

From her they learned the wrongs they ought to shun,
What things to love, what work must still be done.
She led them through the labyrinth of youth
And brought five men and women up to truth.

She mothered five!
Her name may be unknown save to the few;
Of her the outside world but little knew;
But somewhere five are treading virtue's ways,
Serving the world and brightening its days;
Somewhere are five, who, tempted, stand upright,
Who cling to honor, keep her memory bright;
Somewhere this mother toils and is alive
No more as one, but in the breasts of five.

LITTLE GIRLS ARE BEST

Little girls are mighty nice,
    Take 'em any way they come;
They are always worth their price;
    Life without 'em would be glum;
Run earth's lists of treasures through,
    Pile 'em high until they fall,
Gold an' costly jewels, too—
    Little girls are best of all.

Nothing equals 'em on earth!
    I'm an old man an' I know
Any little girl is worth
    More than all the gold below;
Eyes o' blue or brown or gray,
    Raven hair or golden curls,
There's no joy on earth today
    Quite so fine as little girls.

Pudgy nose or freckled face,
    Fairy-like or plain to see,
God has surely blessed the place
    Where a little girl may be;
They're the jewels of His crown
    Dropped to earth from heaven above,
Like wee angel souls sent down
    To remind us of His love.

God has made some lovely things—
    Roses red an' skies o' blue,
Trees an' babbling silver springs,
    Gardens glistening with dew—
But take every gift to man,
    Big an' little, great an' small,
Judge it on its merits, an'
    Little girls are best of all!

THE WORLD AND BUD

If we were all alike, what a dreadful world 'twould be!
No one would know which one was you or which of us was me.
We'd never have a "Skinny" or a "Freckles" or a "Fat,"
An' there wouldn't be a sissy boy to wear a velvet hat;
An' we'd all of us be pitchers when we played a baseball match,
For we'd never have a feller who'd have nerve enough to catch.

If we were all alike an' looked an' thought the same,
I wonder how'd they call us, 'cause there'd only be one name.
An' there'd only be one flavor for our ice cream sodas, too,
An' one color for a necktie an' I 'spose that would be blue;
An' maybe we'd have mothers who were very fond of curls,
An' they'd make us fellers wear our hair like lovely little girls.

Sometimes I think it's funny when I hear some feller say
That he isn't fond of chocolate, when I eat it every day.
Or some other fellow doesn't like the books I like to read;
But I'm glad that we are different, yes, siree! I am indeed.
If everybody looked alike an' talked alike, Oh, Gee!
We'd never know which one was you or which of us was me.

AW GEE WHIZ!

Queerest little chap he is,
Always saying: "Aw Gee Whiz!"
Needing something from the store
That you've got to send him for
And you call him from his play,
Then it is you hear him say:
      "Aw Gee Whiz!"

Seems that most expressive phrase
Is a part of childhood days;
Call him in at supper time,
Hands and face all smeared with grime,
Send him up to wash, and he
Answers you disgustedly:
      "Aw Gee Whiz!"

When it's time to go to bed
And he'd rather play instead,
As you call him from the street,
He comes in with dragging feet,
Knowing that he has to go,
Then it is he mutters low:
      "Aw Gee Whiz!"

Makes no difference what you ask
Of him as a little task;
He has yet to learn that life
Crosses many a joy with strife,
So when duty mars his play,
Always we can hear him say:
     "Aw Gee Whiz!"

PRACTICING TIME

Always whenever I want to play
I've got to practice an hour a day,
Get through breakfast an' make my bed,
And Mother says: "Marjorie, run ahead!
There's a time for work and a time for fun,
So go and get your practicing done."
And Bud, he chuckles and says to me:
"Yes, do your practicing, Marjorie."
A brother's an awful tease, you know,
And he just says that 'cause I hate it so.

They leave me alone in the parlor there
To play the scales or "The Maiden's Prayer,"
And if I stop, Mother's bound to call,
"Marjorie dear, you're not playing at all!
Don't waste your time, but keep right on,
Or you'll have to stay when the hour is gone."
Or maybe the maid looks in at me
And says: "You're not playing, as I can see.
Just hustle along—I've got work to do
And I can't dust the room until you get through."

Then when I've run over the scales and things
Like "The Fairies' Dance," or "The Mountain Springs,"
And my fingers ache and my head is sore,

I find I must sit there a half hour more.
An hour is terribly long, I say,
When you've got to practice and want to play.
So slowly at times has the big hand dropped
That I was sure that the clock had stopped,
But Mother called down to me: "Don't forget—
A full hour, please. It's not over yet."

Oh, when I get big and have children, too,
There's one thing that I will never do—
I won't have brothers to tease the girls
And make them mad when they pull their curls
And laugh at them when they've got to stay
And practice their music an hour a day;
I won't have a maid like the one we've got,
That likes to boss you around a lot;
And I won't have a clock that can go so slow
When it's practice time, 'cause I hate it so.

THE CHRISTMAS GIFT FOR MOTHER

In the Christmas times of the long ago,
There was one event we used to know
   That was better than any other;
It wasn't the toys that we hoped to get,
But the talks we had—and I hear them yet—
   Of the gift we'd buy for Mother.

If ever love fashioned a Christmas gift,
Or saved its money and practiced thrift,
   'Twas done in those days, my brother—
Those golden times of Long Gone By,
Of our happiest years, when you and I
   Talked over the gift for Mother.

We hadn't gone forth on our different ways
Nor coined our lives into yesterdays
   In the fires that smelt and smother,
And we whispered and planned in our youthful glee
Of that marvelous "something" which was to be
   The gift of our hearts to Mother.

It had to be all that our purse could give,
Something she'd treasure while she could live,
   And better than any other.

We gave it the best of our love and thought,
And, Oh, the joy when at last we'd bought
  That marvelous gift for Mother!

Now I think as we go on our different ways,
Of the joy of those vanished yesterdays.
  How good it would be, my brother,
If this Christmas-time we could only know
That same sweet thrill of the Long Ago
  When we shared in the gift for Mother.

BEDTIME

It's bedtime, and we lock the door,
Put out the lights—the day is o'er;
All that can come of good or ill,
The record of this day to fill,
Is written down; the worries cease,
And old and young may rest in peace.

We knew not when we started out
What dangers hedged us all about,
What little pleasures we should gain,
What should be ours to bear of pain.
But now the fires are burning low,
And this day's history we know.

No harm has come. The laughter here
Has been unbroken by a tear;
We've met no hurt too great to bear,
We have not had to bow to care;
The children all are safe in bed,
There's nothing now for us to dread.

When bedtime comes and we can say
That we have safely lived the day.
How sweet the calm that settles down

And shuts away the noisy town!
There is no danger now to fear
Until tomorrow shall appear.

When the long bedtime comes, and I
In sleep eternal come to lie—
When life has nothing more in store,
And silently I close the door,
God grant my weary soul may claim
Security from hurt and shame.

THE WILLING HORSE

I'd rather be the willing horse that people ride to death
Than be the proud and haughty steed that children dare not touch;
I'd rather haul a merry pack and finish out of breath
Than never leave the barn to toil because I'm worth too much.
So boast your noble pedigrees
And talk of manners, if you please—
The weary horse enjoys his ease
    When all his work is done;
The willing horse, day in and out,
Can hear the merry children shout
And every time they are about
    He shares in all their fun.

I want no guards beside my door to pick and choose my friends for me;
I would not be shut off from men as is the fancy steed;
I do not care when I go by that no one turns his eyes to see
The dashing manner of my gait which marks my noble breed;
I am content to trudge the road
And willingly to draw my load—
Sometimes to know the spur and goad
    When I begin to lag;
I'd rather feel the collar jerk
And tug at me, the while I work,
Than all the tasks of life to shirk
    As does the stylish nag.

So let me be the willing horse that now and then is overtasked,
Let me be one the children love and freely dare to ride—
I'd rather be the gentle steed of which too much is sometimes asked
Than be the one that never knows the youngsters at his side.
So drive me wheresoe'er you will,
On level road or up the hill,
Pile on my back the burdens still
    And run me out of breath—
In love and friendship, day by day,
And kindly words I'll take my pay;
A willing horse; that is the way
    I choose to meet my death.

WHERE CHILDREN PLAY

On every street there's a certain place
Where the children gather to romp and race;
There's a certain house where they meet in throngs
To play their games and to sing their songs,
And they trample the lawn with their busy feet
And they scatter their playthings about the street,
But though some folks order them off, I say,
Let the house be mine where the children play.

Armies gather about the door
And fill the air with their battle roar;
Cowboys swinging their lariat loops
Dash round the house with the wildest whoops,
And old folks have to look out when they
Are holding an Indian tribe at bay,
For danger may find them on flying feet,
Who pass by the house where the children meet.

There are lawns too lovely to bear the weight
Of a troop of boys when they roller skate;
There are porches fine that must never know
The stamping of footsteps that come and go,
But on every street there's a favorite place
Where the children gather to romp and race,
And I'm glad in my heart that it's mine to say
Ours is the house where the children play.

HOW DO YOU BUY YOUR MONEY?

How do you buy your money? For money is bought and sold,
And each man barters himself on earth for his silver and shining gold,
And by the bargain he makes with men, the sum of his life is told.

Some buy their coins in a manly way, some buy them with honest toil;
Some pay for their currency here on earth by tilling a patch of soil;
Some buy it with copper and iron and steel, and some with barrels of oil.

The good man buys it from day to day by giving the best he can;
He coins his strength for his children's needs and lives to a simple plan,
And he keeps some time for the home he makes and some for his
    fellowman.

But some men buy it with women's tears, and some with a blasted name;
And some will barter the joy of life for the fortune they hope to claim;
And some are so mad for the clink of gold that they buy it with deeds
    of shame.

How do you buy your money? For money demands its price,
And some men think when they purchase coin that they mustn't be over-
    nice—
But beware of the man who would sell you gold at a shameful sacrifice!

MOTHER'S DAY

Let every day be Mother's Day!
Make roses grow along her way
   And beauty everywhere.
Oh, never let her eyes be wet
With tears of sorrow or regret,
   And never cease to care!
Come, grown up children, and rejoice
That you can hear your mother's voice!

A day for her! For you she gave
Long years of love and service brave;
   For you her youth was spent.
There was no weight of hurt or care
Too heavy for her strength to bear;
   She followed where you went;
Her courage and her love sublime
You could depend on all the time.

No day or night she set apart
On which to open wide her heart
   And welcome you within;
There was no hour you would not be

First in her thought and memory,
　　Though you were black as sin!
Though skies were gray or skies were blue
Not once has she forgotten you.

Let every day be Mother's Day!
With love and roses strew her way,
　　And smiles of joy and pride!
Come, grown up children, to the knee
Where long ago you used to be
　　And never turn aside;
Oh, never let her eyes grow wet
With tears, because her babes forget.

WHEN WE PLAY THE FOOL

Last night I stood in a tawdry place
And watched the ways of the human race.
I looked at a party of shrieking girls
Piled on a table that whirls and whirls,
And saw them thrown in a tangled heap,
Sprawling and squirming and several deep.
And unto the wife who was standing by,
"These are all angels to be," said I.

I followed the ways of the merry throng
And heard the laughter and mirth and song.
Into a barrel which turned and swayed
Men and women a journey made,
And tumbling together they seemed to be
Like so many porpoises out at sea—
Men and women who'd worked all day,
Eagerly seeking a chance to play.

"What do you make of it all?" she said.
I answered: "The dead are a long time dead,
And care is bitter and duty stern,
And each must weep when it comes his turn.
And all grow weary and long for play,
So here is laughter to end the day.
Foolish? Oh, yes, it is that," said I,
"But better the laugh than the dreary sigh.

"Now look at us here, for we're like them, too,
And many the foolish things we do.
We often grow silly and seek a smile
In a thousand ways that are not worth while;
Yet after the mirth and the jest are through,
We shall all be judged by the deeds we do,
And God shall forget on the Judgment Day
The fools we were in our hours of play."

WHAT MAKES AN ARTIST

We got to talking art one day, discussing in a general way
How some can match with brush and paint the glory of a tree,
And some in stone can catch the things of which the dreamy poet
    sings,
While others seem to have no way to tell the joys they see.

Old Blake had sat in silence there and let each one of us declare
Our notions of what's known as art, until he'd heard us through;
And then said he: "It seems to me that any man, whoe'er he be,
Becomes an artist by the good he daily tries to do.

"He need not write the books men read to be an artist. No, indeed!
He need not work with paint and brush to show his love of art;
Who does a kindly deed today and helps another on his way,
Has painted beauty on a face and played the poet's part.

"Though some of us cannot express our inmost thoughts of loveliness,
We prove we love the beautiful by how we act and live;
The poet singing of a tree no greater poet is than he
Who finds it in his heart some care unto a tree to give.

"Though he who works in marble stone the name of artist here may own,
No less an artist is the man who guards his children well;
'Tis art to love the fine and true; by what we are and what we do
How much we love life's nobler things to all the world we tell."

SHE POWDERS HER NOSE

A woman is queer, there's no doubt about that.
She hates to be thin and she hates to be fat;
One minute it's laughter, the next it's a cry—
You can't understand her, however you try;
But there's one thing about her which everyone knows—
A woman's not dressed till she powders her nose.

You never can tell what a woman will say;
She's a law to herself every hour of the day.
It keeps a man guessing to know what to do,
And mostly he's wrong when his guessing is through;
But this you can bet on, wherever she goes
She'll find some occasion to powder her nose.

I've studied the sex for a number of years;
I've watched her in laughter and seen her in tears;
On her ways and her whims I have pondered a lot,
To find what will please her and just what will not;
But all that I've learned from the start to the close
Is that sooner or later she'll powder her nose.

At church or a ball game, a dance or a show,
There's one thing about her I know that I know—
At weddings or funerals, dinners of taste,
You can bet that her hand will dive into her waist,
And every few minutes she'll strike up a pose,
And the whole world must wait till she powders her nose.

THE CHIP ON YOUR SHOULDER

You'll learn when you're older that chip on your shoulder
    Which you dare other boys to upset,
And stand up and fight for and struggle and smite for,
    Has caused you much shame and regret.
When Time, life's adviser, has made you much wiser,
    You won't be so quick with the blow;
You won't be so willing to fight for a shilling,
    And change a good friend to a foe.

You won't be a sticker for trifles, and bicker
    And quarrel for nothing at all;
You'll grow to be kinder, more thoughtful and blinder
    To faults which are petty and small.
You won't take the trouble your two fists to double
    When someone your pride may offend;
When with rage now you bristle you'll smile or you'll whistle,
    And keep the good will of a friend.

You'll learn when you're older that chip on your shoulder
    Which proudly you battle to guard,
Has frequently shamed you and often defamed you
    And left you a record that's marred!
When you've grown calm and steady, you won't be so ready
    To fight for a difference that's small,
For you'll know, when you're older that chip on your shoulder
    Is only a chip after all.

ALL FOR THE BEST

Things mostly happen for the best.
However hard it seems today,
When some fond plan has gone astray
Or what you've wished for most is lost
An' you sit countin' up the cost
With eyes half-blind by tears o' grief
While doubt is chokin' out belief,
You'll find when all is understood
That what seemed bad was really good.

Life can't be counted in a day.
The present rain that will not stop
Next autumn means a bumper crop.
We wonder why some things must be—
Care's purpose we can seldom see—
An' yet long afterwards we turn
To view the past, an' then we learn
That what once filled our minds with doubt
Was good for us as it worked out.

I've never known an hour of care
But that I've later come to see
That it has brought some joy to me.
Even the sorrows I have borne,
Leavin' me lonely an' forlorn

An' hurt an' bruised an' sick at heart,
In life's great plan have had a part.
An' though I could not understand
Why I should bow to Death's command,
As time went on I came to know
That it was really better so.

Things mostly happen for the best.
So narrow is our vision here
That we are blinded by a tear
An' stunned by every hurt an' blow
Which comes today to strike us low.
An' yet some day we turn an' find
That what seemed cruel once was kind.
Most things, I hold, are wisely planned
If we could only understand.

THE KICK UNDER THE TABLE

After a man has been married awhile,
And his wife has grown used to his manner and style,
When she knows from the twinkle that lights up his eye
The thoughts he is thinking, the wherefore and why,
And just what he'll say, and just what he'll do,
And is sure that he'll make a bad break ere he's through,
She has one little trick that she'll work when she's able—
She takes a sly kick at him under the table.

He may fancy the story he's telling is true,
Or he's doing the thing which is proper to do;
He may fancy he's holding his own with the rest,
The life of the party and right at his best,
When quickly he learns to his utter dismay,
That he mustn't say what he's just started to say.
He is stopped at the place where he hoped to begin,
By his wife, who has taken a kick at his shin.

If he picks the wrong fork for the salad, he knows
That fact by the feel of his wife's slippered toes.
If he's started a bit of untellable news,
On the calf of his leg there is planted a bruise.
Oh, I wonder sometimes what would happen to me
If the wife were not seated just where she could be
On guard every minute to watch every trick,
And keep me in line all the time with her kick.

LEADER OF THE GANG

Seems only just a year ago that he was toddling round the place
In pretty little colored suits and with a pink and shining face.
I used to hold him in my arms to watch when our canary sang,
And now tonight he tells me that he's leader of his gang.

It seems but yesterday, I vow, that I with fear was almost dumb,
Living those dreadful hours of care waiting the time for him to come;
And I can still recall the thrill of that first cry of his which rang
Within our walls. And now that babe tells me he's leader of his gang.

Gone from our lives are all the joys which yesterday we used to own;
The baby that we thought we had, out of the little home has flown,
And in his place another stands, whose garments in disorder hang,
A lad who now with pride proclaims that he's the leader of his gang.

And yet somehow I do not grieve for what it seems we may have lost;
To have so strong a boy as this, most cheerfully I pay the cost.
I find myself a sense of joy to comfort every little pang,
And pray that they shall find in him a worthy leader of the gang.

MA AND THE OUIJA BOARD

I don't know what it's all about, but Ma says that she wants to know
If spirits in the other world can really talk to us below.
An' Pa says, "Gosh! there's folks enough on earth to talk to, I should think,
Without you pesterin' the folks whose souls have gone across the brink."
But Ma, she wants to find out things an' study on her own accord,
An' so a month or two ago she went an' bought a ouija board.

It's just a shiny piece of wood, with letters printed here an' there,
An' has a little table which you put your fingers on with care,
An' then you sit an' whisper low some question that you want to know.
Then by an' by the spirit comes an' makes the little table go,
An' Ma, she starts to giggle then an' Pa just grumbles out, "Oh, Lord!
I wish you hadn't bought this thing. We didn't need a ouija board."

"You're movin' it!" says Ma to Pa. "I'm not!" says Pa, "I know it's you;
You're makin' it spell things to us that you know very well aren't true."
"That isn't so," says Ma to him, "but I am certain from the way
The ouija moves that you're the one who's tellin' it just what to say."
"It's just 'lectricity," says Pa; "like batteries all men are stored,
But anyhow I don't believe we ought to have a ouija board."

One night Ma got it out, an' said, "Now, Pa, I want you to be fair,
Just keep right still an' let your hands rest lightly on the table there.
Oh, Ouija, tell me, tell me true, are we to buy another car,
An' will we get it very soon?" she asked. "Oh, tell us from afar."
"Don't buy a car," the letters spelled, "the price this year you can't afford."
Then Ma got mad, an' since that time she's never used the ouija board.

THE CALL OF THE WOODS

I must get out to the woods again, to the whispering trees and the birds
    awing,
Away from the haunts of pale-faced men, to the spaces wide where
    strength is king;
I must get out where the skies are blue and the air is clean and the rest is
    sweet,
Out where there's never a task to do or a goal to reach or a foe to meet.

I must get out on the trails once more that wind through shadowy haunts
    and cool,
Away from the presence of wall and door, and see myself in a crystal
    pool;
I must get out with the silent things, where neither laughter nor hate is
    heard,
Where malice never the humblest stings and no one is hurt by a spoken
    word.

Oh, I've heard the call of the tall white pine, and heard the call of the
    running brook;
I'm tired of the tasks which each day are mine; I'm weary of reading a
    printed book.
I want to get out of the din and strife, the clang and clamor of turning
    wheel,
And walk for a day where life is life, and the joys are true and the pictures
    real.

COMMITTEE MEETINGS

For this and that and various things
    It seems that men must get together,
To purchase cups or diamond rings
    Or to discuss the price of leather.
From nine to ten, or two to three,
    Or any hour that's fast and fleeting,
There is a constant call for me
    To go to some committee meeting.

The church has serious work to do,
    The lodge and club has need of workers,
They ask for just an hour or two—
    Surely I will not join the shirkers?
Though I have duties of my own
    I should not drop before completing,
There comes the call by telephone
    To go to some committee meeting.

No longer may I eat my lunch
    In quietude and contemplation;
I must foregather with the bunch
    To raise a fund to save the nation.
And I must talk of plans and schemes
    The while a scanty bite I'm eating,
Until I vow today it seems
    My life is one committee meeting.

148

When over me the night shall fall,
    And my poor soul goes upwards winging
Unto that heavenly realm, where all
    Is bright with joy and gay with singing,
I hope to hear St. Peter say—
    And I shall thank him for the greeting:
"Come in and rest from day to day;
    Here there is no committee meeting!"

PA AND THE MONTHLY BILLS

When Ma gets out the monthly bills and sets them all in front of Dad,
She makes us children run away because she knows he may get mad;
An' then she smiles a bit and says: "I hope you will not fuss and fret—
There's nothing here except the things I absolutely had to get!"
An' Pa he looks 'em over first. "The things you had to have!" says he;
"I s'pose that we'd have died without that twenty dollar longeree."

Then he starts in to write the checks for laundry an' for light an' gas,
An' never says a word 'bout them—because they're small he lets 'em
    pass.
But when he starts to grunt an' groan, an' stops the while his pipe he
    fills,
We know that he is gettin' down to where Ma's hid the bigger bills.
"Just what we had to have," says he, "an' I'm supposed to pay the tolls;
Nine dollars an' a half for—say, what the deuce are camisoles?

"If you should break a leg," says Pa, "an couldn't get down town to
    shop,
I'll bet the dry goods men would see their business take an awful drop,
An' if they missed you for a week, they'd have to fire a dozen clerks!
Say, couldn't we have got along without this bunch of Billie Burkes?"
But Ma just sits an' grins at him, an' never has a word to say,
Because she says Pa likes to fuss about the bills he has to pay.

BOB WHITE

Out near the links where I go to play
My favorite game from day to day,
There's a friend of mine that I've never met
Walked with or broken bread with, yet
I've talked to him oft and he's talked to me
Whenever I've been where he's chanced to be;
He's a cheery old chap who keeps out of sight,
A gay little fellow whose name is Bob White.

Bob White! Bob White! I can hear him call
As I follow the trail to my little ball—
Bob White! Bob White! with a note of cheer
That was just designed for a mortal ear.
Then I drift far off from the world of men
And I send an answer right back to him then;
An' we whistle away to each other there,
Glad of the life which is ours to share.

Bob White! Bob White! May you live to be
The head of a numerous family!
May you boldly call to your friends out here,
With never an enemy's gun to fear.
I'm a better man as I pass along,
For your cheery call and your bit of song.
May your food be plenty and skies be bright
To the end of your days, good friend Bob White!

WHEN MA WANTS SOMETHING NEW

Last night Ma said to Pa: "My dear,
The Williamsons are coming here
To visit for a week or two,
An' I must have a talk with you.
We need some things which we must get—
You promised me a dinner set,
An' I should like it while they're here."
An' Pa looked up an' said: "My dear,
A dinner set? Well, I guess not.
What's happened to the one we've got?"

"We need a parlor rug," says Ma.
"We've got a parlor rug," says Pa.
"We ought to have another chair."
"You're sittin' in a good one there."
"The parlor curtains are a fright."
"When these are washed they look all right."
"The old stuff's pitiful to see."
"It still looks mighty good to me."
"The sofa's worn beyond repair."
"It doesn't look so bad, I swear."

"Gee Whiz, you make me tired," says Ma.
"Why, what's the matter now?" says Pa.
"You come an' go an' never see

How old our stuff has grown to be;
It still looks just the same to you
As what it did when it was new,
An' every time you think it strange
That I should like to have a change."
"I'm gettin' old," says Pa. "Maybe
You'd like a younger man than me."

"If this old rug was worn an' thin,
At night you'd still come walkin' in
An' throw your hat upon a chair
An' never see a single tear;
So long as any chair could stand
An' bear your weight you'd think it grand.
If home depended all on you,
It never would get something new."
"All right," says Pa, "go buy the stuff!
But, say, am I still good enough?"

SITTIN' ON THE PORCH

Sittin' on the porch at night when all the tasks are done,
Just restin' there an' talkin', with my easy slippers on,
An' my shirt band thrown wide open an' my feet upon the rail,
Oh, it's then I'm at my richest, with a wealth that cannot fail;
For the scent of early roses seems to flood the evening air,
An' a throne of downright gladness is my wicker rocking chair.

The dog asleep beside me, an' the children rompin' 'round
With their shrieks of merry laughter, Oh, there is no gladder sound
To the ears o' weary mortals, spite of all the scoffers say,
Or a grander bit of music than the children at their play!
An' I tell myself times over, when I'm sittin' there at night,
That the world in which I'm livin' is a place o' real delight.

Then the moon begins its climbin' an' the stars shine overhead,
An' the mother calls the children an' she takes 'em up to bed,
An' I smoke my pipe in silence an' I think o' many things,
An' balance up my riches with the lonesomeness o' kings,
An' I come to this conclusion, an' I'll wager that I'm right—
That I'm happier than they are, sittin' on my porch at night.

WITH DOG AND GUN

Out in the woods with a dog an' gun
Is my idea of a real day's fun.
'Tain't the birds that I'm out to kill
That furnish me with the finest thrill,
'Cause I never worry or fret a lot,
Or curse my luck if I miss a shot.
There's many a time, an' I don't know why,
That I shoot too low or I aim too high,
An' all I can see is the distant whirr
Of a bird that's gittin' back home to her—
Yep, gittin' back home at the end o' day,
An' I'm just as glad that he got away.

There's a whole lot more in the woods o' fall
Than the birds you bag—if you think at all.
There's colors o' gold an' red an' brown
As never were known in the busy town;
There's room to breathe in the purest air
An' something worth looking at everywhere;
There's the dog who's leadin' you on an' on
To a patch o' cover where birds have gone,
An' standin' there, without move or change,
Till you give the sign that you've got the range.
That's thrill enough for my blood, I say,
So why should I care if they get away?

Fact is, there are times that I'd ruther miss
Than to bring 'em down, 'cause I feel like this:
There's a heap more joy in a living thing
Than a breast crushed in or a broken wing,
An' I can't feel right, an' I never will,
When I look at a bird that I've dared to kill.
Oh, I'm jus' plumb happy to tramp about
An' follow my dog as he hunts 'em out,
Jus' watchin' him point in his silent way
Where the Bob Whites are an' the partridge stay;
For the joy o' the great outdoors I've had,
So why should I care if my aim is bad?

OLD MISTER LAUGHTER

Old Mister Laughter
    Comes a-grinnin' down the way,
Singin': "Never mind your troubles,
    For they'll surely pass away."
Singin': "Now the sun is shinin'
    An' there's roses everywhere;
Tomorrow will be soon enough
    To fret about your care."

Old Mister Laughter
    Comes a-grinnin' at my door,
Singin': "Don't go after money
    When you've got enough and more."
Singin': "Laugh with me this mornin'
    An' be happy while you may.
What's the use of riches
    If they never let you play?"

Old Mister Laughter
    Comes a-grinnin' all the time,
Singin' happy songs o' gladness
    In a good old-fashioned rhyme.
Singin': "Keep the smiles a-goin',
    Till they write your epitaph,
And don't let fame or fortune
    Ever steal away your laugh."

A FAMILY ROW

I freely confess there are good friends of mine,
With whom we are often invited to dine,
Who get on my nerves so that I cannot eat
Or stay with my usual ease in my seat;
For I know that if something should chance to occur
Which he may not like or which doesn't please her,
That we'll have to try to be pleasant somehow
While they stage a fine little family row.

Now a family row is a private affair,
And guests, I am certain, should never be there;
I have freely maintained that a man and his wife
Cannot always agree on their journey through life,
But they ought not to bicker and wrangle and shout
And show off their rage when their friends are about;
It takes all the joy from a party, I vow,
When some couple starts up a family row.

It's a difficult job to stay cool and polite
When your host and your hostess are staging a fight:
It's hard to talk sweet to a dame with a frown
Or smile at a man that you want to knock down.
You sit like a dummy and look far away,
But you just can't help hearing the harsh things they say.
It ruins the dinner, I'm telling you now,
When your host and your hostess get mixed in a row.

THE LUCKY MAN

Luck had a favor to bestow
And wondered where to let it go.

"No lazy man on earth," said she,
"Shall get this happy gift from me.

"I will not pass it to the man
Who will not do the best he can.

"I will not make this splendid gift
To one who has not practiced thrift.

"It shall not benefit deceit,
Nor help the man who's played the cheat.

"He that has failed to fight with pluck
Shall never know the Goddess Luck.

"I'll look around a bit to see
What man has earned some help from me."

She found a man whose hands were soiled
Because from day to day he'd toiled.

He'd dreamed by night and worked by day
To make life's contest go his way.

He'd kept his post and daily slaved,
And something of his wage he'd saved.

He'd clutched at every circumstance
Which might have been his golden chance.

The goddess smiled and then, kerslap!
She dropped her favor in his lap.

LONELY

They're all away
   And the house is still,
And the dust lies thick
   On the window sill,
And the stairway creaks
   In a solemn tone
This taunting phrase:
   "You are all alone."

They've gone away
   And the rooms are bare;
I miss his cap
   From a parlor chair.
And I miss the toys
   In the lonely hall,
But most of any
   I miss his call.

I miss the shouts
   And the laughter gay
Which greeted me
   At the close of day,
And there isn't a thing
   In the house we own
But sobbingly says:
   "You are all alone."

It's only a house
    That is mine to know,
An empty house
    That is cold with woe;
Like a prison grim
    With its bars of black,
And it won't be home
    Till they all come back.

THE COOKIE JAR

You can rig up a house with all manner of things,
The prayer rugs of sultans and princes and kings;
You can hang on its walls the old tapestries rare
Which some dead Egyptian once treasured with care;
But though costly and gorgeous its furnishings are,
It must have, to be homelike, an old cookie jar.

There are just a few things that a home must possess,
Besides all your money and all your success—
A few good old books which some loved one has read,
Some trinkets of those whose sweet spirits have fled,
And then in the pantry, not shoved back too far
For the hungry to get to, that old cookie jar.

Let the house be a mansion, I care not at all!
Let the finest of pictures be hung on each wall,
Let the carpets be made of the richest velour,
And the chairs only those which great wealth can procure,
I'd still want to keep for the joy of my flock
That homey, old-fashioned, well-filled cookie crock.

Like the love of the Mother it shines through our years;
It has soothed all our hurts and has dried away tears;
It has paid us for toiling; in sorrow or joy,
It has always shown kindness to each girl and boy;
And I'm sorry for people, whoever they are,
Who live in a house where there's no cookie jar.

LITTLE WRANGLES

Lord, we've had our little wrangles, an' we've had our little bouts;
There's many a time, I reckon, that we have been on the outs;
My tongue's a trifle hasty an' my temper's apt to fly,
An' Mother, let me tell you, has a sting in her reply,
But I couldn't live without her, an' it's plain as plain can be
That in fair or sunny weather Mother needs a man like me.

I've banged the door an' muttered angry words beneath my breath,
For at times when she was scoldin' Mother's plagued me most to death,
But we've always laughed it over, when we'd both cooled down a bit,
An' we never had a difference but a smile would settle it.
An' if such a thing could happen, we could share life's joys an' tears
An' live right on together for another thousand years.

Some men give up too easy in the game o' married life;
They haven't got the courage to be worthy of a wife;
An' I've seen a lot o' women that have made their lives a mess,
'Cause they couldn't bear the burdens that are, mixed with happiness.
So long as folks are human they'll have many faults that jar,
An' the way to live with people is to take them as they are.

We've been forty years together, good an' bad, an' rain an' shine;
I've forgotten Mother's faults now an' she never mentions mine.
In the days when sorrow struck us an' we shared a common woe
We just leaned upon each other, an' our weakness didn't show.
An' I learned how much I need her an' how tender she can be
An' through it, maybe, Mother saw the better side o' me.

THE WIDE OUTDOORS

The rich may pay for orchids rare, but, Oh the apple tree
Flings out its blossoms to the world for every eye to see,
And all who sigh for loveliness may walk beneath the sky
And claim a richer beauty than man's gold can ever buy.

The blooming cherry trees are free for all to look upon;
The dogwood buds for all of us, and not some favorite one;
The wide outdoors is no man's own; the stranger on the street
Can cast his eyes on many a rose and claim its fragrance sweet.

Small gardens are shut in by walls, but none can wall the sky,
And none can hide the friendly trees from all who travel by;
And none can hold the apple boughs and claim them for his own,
For all the beauties of the earth belong to God alone.

So let me walk the world just now and wander far and near;
Earth's loveliness is mine to see, its music mine to hear;
There's not a single apple bough that spills its blooms about
But I can claim the joy of it, and none can shut me out.

"WHERE'S MAMMA?"

Comes in flying from the street;
   "Where's Mamma?"
Friend or stranger thus he'll greet:
   "Where's Mamma?"
Doesn't want to say hello,
Home from school or play he'll go
Straight to what he wants to know:
   "Where's Mamma?"

Many times a day he'll shout,
   "Where's Mamma?"
Seems afraid that she's gone out;
   "Where's Mamma?"
Is his first thought at the door—
She's the one he's looking for,
And he questions o'er and o'er,
   "Where's Mamma?"

Can't be happy till he knows:
   "Where's Mamma?"
So he begs us to disclose
   "Where's Mamma?"
And it often seems to me,
As I hear his anxious plea,
That no sweeter phrase can be:
   "Where's Mamma?"

Like to hear it day by day;
    "Where's Mamma?"
Loveliest phrase that lips can say:
    "Where's Mamma?"
And I pray as time shall flow,
And the long years come and go,
That he'll always want to know
    "Where's Mamma?"

SUMMER DREAMS

Drowsy old summer, with nothing to do,
I'd like to be drowsin' an' dreamin' with you;
I'd like to stretch out in the shade of a tree,
An' fancy the white clouds were ships out at sea,
Or castles with turrets and treasures and things,
And peopled with princesses, fairies and kings,
An' just drench my soul with the glorious joy
Which was mine to possess as a barefooted boy.

Drowsy old summer, your skies are as blue
As the skies which a dreamy-eyed youngster once knew,
An' I fancy today all the pictures are there—
The ships an' the pirates an' princesses fair,
The red scenes of battle, the gay, cheering throngs
Which greeted the hero who righted all wrongs;
But somehow or other, these old eyes of mine
Can't see what they did as a youngster of nine.

Drowsy old summer, I'd like to forget
Some things which I've learned an' some hurts I have met;
I'd like the old visions of splendor an' joy
Which were mine to possess as a barefooted boy
When I dreamed of the glorious deeds I would do
As soon as I'd galloped my brief boyhood through;
I'd like to come back an' look into your skies
With that wondrous belief an' those far-seeing eyes.

Drowsy old summer, my dream days have gone;
Only things which are real I must now look upon;
No longer I see in the skies overhead
The pictures that were, for the last one has fled.
I have learned that not all of our dreams can come true;
That the toilers are many and heroes are few;
But I'd like once again to look up there an' see
The man that I fancied some day I might be.

I AIN'T DEAD YET

Time was I used to worry and I'd sit around an' sigh,
And think with every ache I got that I was goin' to die,
I'd see disaster comin' from a dozen different ways
An' prophesy calamity an' dark and dreary days.
But I've come to this conclusion, that it's foolishness to fret;
I've had my share o' sickness, but I
                    Ain't
                        Dead
                            Yet!

Wet springs have come to grieve me an' I've grumbled at the showers,
But I can't recall a June-time that forgot to bring the flowers.
I've had my business troubles, and looked failure in the face,
But the crashes I expected seemed to pass right by the place.
So I'm takin' life more calmly, pleased with everything I get,
An' not over-hurt by losses, 'cause I
                    Ain't
                        Dead
                            Yet!

I've feared a thousand failures an' a thousand deaths I've died,
I've had this world in ruins by the gloom I've prophesied.
But the sun shines out this mornin' an' the skies above are blue,
An' with all my griefs an' trouble, I have somehow lived 'em through.
There may be cares before me, much like those that I have met;
Death will come some day an' take me, but I

Ain't

Dead

Yet!

THE CURE FOR WEARINESS

Seemed like I couldn't stand it any more,
   The factory whistles blowin' day by day,
An' men an' children hurryin' by the door,
   An' street cars clangin' on their busy way.
The faces of the people seemed to be
   Washed pale by tears o' grief an' strife an' care,
Till everywhere I turned to I could see
   The same old gloomy pictures of despair.

The windows of the shops all looked the same,
   Decked out with stuff their owners wished to sell;
When visitors across our doorway came
   I could recite the tales they'd have to tell.
All things had lost their old-time power to please;
   Dog-tired I was an' irritable, too,
An' so I traded chimney tops for trees,
   An' shingled roof for open skies of blue.

I dropped my tools an' took my rod an' line
   An' tackle box an' left the busy town;
I found a favorite restin' spot of mine
   Where no one seeks for fortune or renown.
I whistled to the birds that flew about,
   An' built a lot of castles in my dreams;
I washed away the stains of care an' doubt
   An' thanked the Lord for woods an' running streams.

I've cooked my meals before an open fire,
  I've had the joy of green smoke in my face,
I've followed for a time my heart's desire
  An' now the path of duty I retrace.
I've had my little fishin' trip, an' go
  Once more contented to the haunts of men;
I'm ready now to hear the whistles blow
  An' see the roofs an' chimney tops again.

TO AN OLD FRIEND

When we have lived our little lives and wandered all their byways
    through,
When we've seen all that we shall see and finished all that we must do,
When we shall take one backward look off yonder where our journey
    ends,
I pray that you shall be as glad as I shall be that we were friends.

Time was we started out to find the treasures and the joys of life;
We sought them in the land of gold through many days of bitter strife.
When we were young we yearned for fame; in search of joy we went
    afar,
Only to learn how very cold and distant all the strangers are.

When we have met all we shall meet and know what destiny has
    planned,
I shall rejoice in that last hour that I have known your friendly hand;
I shall go singing down the way off yonder as my sun descends
As one who's had a happy life, made glorious by the best of friends.

SATISFIED WITH LIFE

I have known the green trees and the skies overhead
And the blossoms of spring and the fragrance they shed;
I have known the blue sea, and the mountains afar
And the song of the pines and the light of a star;
And should I pass now, I could say with a smile
That my pilgrimage here has been well worth my while.

I have known the warm handclasp of friends who were true;
I have shared in their pleasures and wept with them, too;
I have heard the gay laughter which sweeps away care
And none of the comrades I've made could I spare;
And should this be all, I could say ere I go,
That life is worth while just such friendships to know.

I have builded a home where we've loved and been glad;
I have known the rich joy of a girl and a lad;
I have had their caresses through storm and through shine,
And watched them grow lovely, those youngsters of mine;
And I think as I hold them at night on my knee,
That life has been generous surely to me.

AUTUMN EVENINGS

Apples on the table an' the grate-fire blazin' high,
Oh, I'm sure the whole world hasn't any happier man than I;
The Mother sittin' mendin' little stockin's, toe an' knee,
An' tellin' all that's happened through the busy day to me:
Oh, I don't know how to say it, but these cosy autumn nights
Seem to glow with true contentment an' a thousand real delights.

The dog sprawled out before me knows that huntin' days are here,
'Cause he dreams and seems to whimper that a flock o' quail are near;
An' the children playin' checkers till it's time to go to bed,
Callin' me to settle questions whether black is beatin' red;
Oh, these nights are filled with gladness, an' I puff my pipe an' smile,
An' tell myself the struggle an' the work are both worth while.

The flames are full o' pictures that keep dancin' to an' fro,
Bringin' back the scenes o' gladness o' the happy long ago,
An' the whole wide world is silent an' I tell myself just this—
That within these walls I cherish, there is all my world there is!
Can I keep the love abiding in these hearts so close to me,
An' the laughter of these evenings, I shall gain life's victory.

MEMORIAL DAY

These did not pass in selfishness; they died for all mankind;
They died to build a better world for all who stay behind;
And we who hold their memory dear, and bring them flowers today,
Should consecrate ourselves once more to live and die as they.

These were defenders of the faith and guardians of the truth;
That you and I might live and love, they gladly gave their youth;
And we who set this day apart to honor them who sleep
Should pledge ourselves to hold the faith they gave their lives to keep.

If tears are all we shed for them, then they have died in vain;
If flowers are all we bring them now, forgotten they remain;
If by their courage we ourselves to courage are not led,
Then needlessly these graves have closed above our heroes dead.

To symbolize our love with flowers is not enough to do;
We must be brave as they were brave, and true as they were true.
They died to build a better world, and we who mourn today
Should consecrate ourselves once more to live and die as they.

THE HAPPY MAN

If you would know a happy man,
  Go find the fellow who
Has had a bout with trouble grim
  And just come smiling through.

The load is off his shoulders now,
  Where yesterday he frowned
And saw no joy in life, today
  He laughs his way around.

He's done the very thing he thought
  That he could never do;
His sun is shining high today
  And all his skies are blue.

He's stronger than he was before;
  Should trouble come anew
He'll know how much his strength can bear
  And how much he can do.

Today he has the right to smile,
  And he may gaily sing,
For he has conquered where he feared
  The pain of failure's sting.

Comparison has taught him, too,
  The sweetest hours are those
Which follow on the heels of care,
  With laughter and repose.

If you would meet a happy man,
  Go find the fellow who
Has had a bout with trouble grim
  And just come smiling through.

THE SONG OF THE BUILDER

I sink my piers to the solid rock,
    And I send my steel to the sky,
And I pile up the granite, block by block
    Full twenty stories high;
Nor wind nor weather shall wash away
The thing that I've builded, day by day.

Here's something of mine that shall ever stand
    Till another shall tear it down;
Here is the work of my brain and hand,
    Towering above the town.
And the idlers gay in their smug content,
Have nothing to leave for a monument.

Here from my girders I look below
    At the throngs which travel by,
For little that's real will they leave to show
    When it comes their time to die.
But I, when my time of life is through,
Will leave this building for men to view.

Oh, the work is hard and the days are long,
    But hammers are tools for men,
And granite endures and steel is strong,
    Outliving both brush and pen.
And ages after my voice is stilled,
Men shall know I lived by the things I build.

OLD YEARS AND NEW

Old years and new years, all blended into one,
The best of what there is to be, the best of what is gone—
Let's bury all the failures in the dim and dusty past
And keep the smiles of friendship and laughter to the last.

Old years and new years, life's in the making still;
We haven't come to glory yet, but there's the hope we will;
The dead old year was twelve months long, but now from it we're free,
And what's one year of good or bad to all the years to be?

Old years and new years, we need them one and all
To reach the dome of character and build its sheltering wall;
Past failures tried the souls of us, but if their tests we stood.
The sum of what we are to be may yet be counted good.

Old years and new years, with all their pain and strife,
Are but the bricks and steel and stone with which we fashion life;
So put the sin and shame away, and keep the fine and true,
And on the glory of the past let's build the better new.

WHEN WE'RE ALL ALIKE

I've trudged life's highway up and down;
    I've watched the lines of men march by;
I've seen them in the busy town,
    And seen them under country sky;
I've talked with toilers in the ranks,
    And walked with men whose hands were white,
And learned, when closed were stores and banks,
    We're nearly all alike at night.

Just find the wise professor when
    He isn't lost in ancient lore,
And he, like many other men,
    Romps with his children on the floor.
He puts his gravity aside
    To share in innocent delight.
Stripped of position's pomp and pride,
    We're nearly all the same at night.

Serving a common cause, we go
    Unto our separate tasks by day,
And rich or poor or great or low,
    Regardless of their place or pay,
Cherish the common dreams of men—
    A home where love and peace unite.
We serve the self-same end and plan,
    We're all alike when it is night.

Each for his loved ones wants to do
　　His utmost. Brothers are we all,
When we have run the work-day through,
　　In romping with our children small;
Rich men and poor delight in play
　　When care and caste have taken flight.
At home, in all we think and say,
　　We're very much the same at night.

THE THINGS YOU CAN'T FORGET

They ain't much, seen from day to day—
The big elm tree across the way,
The church spire, an' the meetin' place
Lit up by many a friendly face.
You pass 'em by a dozen times
An' never think o' them in rhymes,
Or fit for poet's singin'. Yet
They're all the things you can't forget;
An' they're the things you'll miss some day
If ever you should go away.

The people here ain't much to see—
Jes' common folks like you an' me,
Doin' the ordinary tasks
Which life of everybody asks:
Old Dr. Green, still farin' 'round
To where his patients can be found,
An' Parson Hill, serene o' face,
Carryin' God's message every place,
An' Jim, who keeps the grocery store—
Yet they are folks you'd hunger for.

They seem so plain when close to view—
Bill Barker, an' his brother too,
The Jacksons, men of higher rank
Because they chance to run the bank,
Yet friends to every one round here,
Quiet an' kindly an' sincere,
Not much to sing about or praise,
Livin' their lives in modest ways—
Yet in your memory they'd stay
If ever you should go away.

These are things an' these the men
Some day you'll long to see again.
Now it's so near you scarcely see
The beauty o' that big elm tree,
But some day later on you will
An' wonder if it's standin' still,
An' if the birds return to sing
An' make their nests there every spring.
Mebbe you scorn them now, but they
Will bring you back again some day.

THE MAKING OF FRIENDS

If nobody smiled and nobody cheered and nobody helped us along,
If each every minute looked after himself and good things all went to
the strong,
If nobody cared just a little for you, and nobody thought about me,
And we stood all alone to the battle of life, what a dreary old world it
would be!

If there were no such a thing as a flag in the sky as a symbol of comradeship
here,
If we lived as the animals live in the woods, with nothing held sacred or
dear,
And selfishness ruled us from birth to the end, and never a neighbor had
we,
And never we gave to another in need, what a dreary old world it would
be!

Oh, if we were rich as the richest on earth and strong as the strongest
that lives,
Yet never we knew the delight and the charm of the smile which the
other man gives,
If kindness were never a part of ourselves, though we owned all the land
we could see,
And friendship meant nothing at all to us here, what a dreary old world
it would be!

Life is sweet just because of the friends we have made and the things
which in common we share;
We want to live on not because of ourselves, but because of the people
who care;
It's giving and doing for somebody else—on that all life's splendor
depends,
And the joy of this world, when you've summed it all up, is found in the
making of friends.

THE DEEDS OF ANGER

I used to lose my temper an' git mad an' tear around
An' raise my voice so wimmin folks would tremble at the sound;
I'd do things I was ashamed of when the fit of rage had passed,
An' wish I hadn't done 'em, an' regret 'em to the last;
But I've learned from sad experience how useless is regret,
For the mean things done in anger are the things you can't forget.

'Tain't no use to kiss the youngster once your hand has made him cry;
You'll recall the time you struck him till the very day you die;
He'll forget it an' forgive you an' tomorrow seem the same,
But you'll keep the hateful picture of your sorrow an' your shame,
An' it's bound to rise to taunt you, though you long have squared the
    debt,
For the things you've done in meanness are the things you can't forget.

Lord, I sometimes sit an' shudder when some scene comes back to me,
Which shows me big an' brutal in some act o' tyranny,
When some triflin' thing upset me an' I let my temper fly,
An' was sorry for it after—but it's vain to sit an' sigh.
So I'd be a whole sight happier now my sun begins to set,
If it wasn't for the meanness which I've done an' can't forget.

Now I think I've learned my lesson an' I'm treadin' gentler ways,
An' I try to build my mornings into happy yesterdays;
I don't let my temper spoil 'em in the way I used to do
An' let some splash of anger smear the record when it's through;
I want my memories pleasant, free from shame or vain regret,
Without any deeds of anger which I never can forget.

I'D RATHER BE A FAILURE

I'd rather be a failure than the man who's never tried;
I'd rather seek the mountain-top than always stand aside.
Oh, let me hold some lofty dream and make my desperate fight,
And though I fail I still shall know I tried to serve the right.

The idlers line the ways of life and they are quick to sneer;
They note the failing strength of man and greet it with a jeer;
But there is something deep inside which scoffers fail to view—
They never see the glorious deed the failure tried to do.

Some men there are who never leave the city's well-worn streets;
They never know the dangers grim the bold adventurer meets;
They never seek a better way nor serve a nobler plan;
They never risk with failure to advance the cause of man.

Oh, better 'tis to fail and fall in sorrow and despair,
Than stand where all is safe and sure and never face a care;
Yes, stamp me with the failure's brand and let men sneer at me,
For though I've failed the Lord shall know the man I tried to be.

COULDN'T LIVE WITHOUT YOU

You're just a little fellow with a lot of funny ways,
Just three-foot-six of mischief set with eyes that fairly blaze;
You're always up to something with those busy hands o' yours,
And you leave a trail o' ruin on the walls an' on the doors,
An' I wonder, as I watch you, an' your curious tricks I see,
Whatever is the reason that you mean so much to me.

You're just a chubby rascal with a grin upon your face,
Just seven years o' gladness, an' a hard and trying case;
You think the world's your playground, an' in all you say an' do
You fancy everybody ought to bow an' scrape to you;
Dull care's a thing you laugh at just as though 'twill never be,
So I wonder, little fellow, why you mean so much to me.

Now your face is smeared with candy or perhaps it's only dirt,
An' it's really most alarming how you tear your little shirt;
But I have to smile upon you, an' with all your wilful ways,
I'm certain that I need you 'round about me all my days;
Yes, I've got to have you with me, for somehow it's come to be
That I couldn't live without you, for you're all the world to me.

JUST A BOY

Get to understand the lad—
He's not eager to be bad;
If the right he always knew,
He would be as old as you.
Were he now exceeding wise,
He'd be just about your size;
When he does things that annoy,
Don't forget, he's just a boy.

Could he know and understand,
He would need no guiding hand;
But he's young and hasn't learned
How life's corners must be turned;
Doesn't know from day to day
There is more in life than play,
More to face than selfish joy—
Don't forget he's just a boy.

Being just a boy, he'll do
Much you will not want him to;
He'll be careless of his ways,
Have his disobedient days,
Wilful, wild and headstrong, too,
Just as, when a boy, were you;
Things of value he'll destroy,
But, reflect, he's just a boy.

Just a boy who needs a friend,
Patient, kindly to the end,
Needs a father who will show
Him the things he wants to know;
Take him with you when you walk,
Listen when he wants to talk,
His companionship enjoy,
Don't forget, he's just a boy!

WHAT HOME'S INTENDED FOR

When the young folks gather 'round in the good old-fashioned way,
Singin' all the latest songs gathered from the newest play,
Or they start the phonograph an' shove the chairs back to the wall
An' hold a little party dance, I'm happiest of all.
Then I sorter settle back, plumb contented to the core,
An' I tell myself most proudly, that's what home's intended for.

When the laughter's gaily ringin' an' the room is filled with song,
I like, to sit an' watch 'em, all that glad an' merry throng,
For the ragtime they are playin' on the old piano there
Beats any high-toned music where the bright lights shine an' glare,
An' the racket they are makin' stirs my pulses more and more,
So I whisper in my gladness: that's what home's intended for.

Then I smile an' say to Mother, let 'em move the chairs about,
Let 'em frolic in the parlor, let 'em shove the tables out,
Jus' so long as they are near us, jus' so long as they will stay
By the fireplace we are keepin', harm will never come their way,
An' you'll never hear me grumble at the bills that keep me poor,
It's the finest part o' livin'—that's what home's intended for.

SAFE AT HOME

Let the old fire blaze
    An' the youngsters shout
An' the dog on the rug
    Sprawl full length out,
An' Mother an' I
    Sort o' settle down—
An' it's little we care
    For the noisy town.

Oh, it's little we care
    That the wind may blow,
An' the streets grow white
    With the drifted snow;
We'll face the storm
    With the break o' day,
But tonight we'll dream
    An' we'll sing an' play.

We'll sit by the fire
    Where it's snug an' warm,
An' pay no heed
    To the winter storm;
With a sheltering roof
    Let the blizzard roar;
We are safe at home—
    Can a king say more?

That's all that counts
    When the day is done:
The smiles of love
    And the youngsters' fun,
The cares put down
    With the evening gloam—
Here's the joy of all:
    To be safe at home.

WHEN FRIENDS DROP IN

It may be I'm old-fashioned, but the times I like the best
Are not the splendid parties with the women gaily dressed,
And the music tuned for dancing and the laughter of the throng,
With a paid comedian's antics or a hired musician's song,
But the quiet times of friendship, with the chuckles and the grin,
And the circle at the fireside when a few good friends drop in.

There's something 'round the fireplace that no club can imitate,
And no throng can ever equal just a few folks near the grate;
Though I sometimes like an opera, there's no music quite so sweet
As the singing of the neighbors that you're always glad to meet;
Oh, I know when they come calling that the fun will soon begin,
And I'm happiest those evenings when a few good friends drop in.

There's no pomp of preparation, there's no style or sham or fuss;
We are glad to welcome callers who are glad to be with us,
And we sit around and visit or we start a merry game,
And we show them by our manner that we're mighty pleased they came,
For there's something real about it, and the yarns we love to spin,
And the time flies, Oh, so swiftly when a few good friends drop in.

Let me live my life among them, cheerful, kindly folks and true,
And I'll ask no greater glory till my time of life is through;
Let me share the love and favor of the few who know me best,
And I'll spend my time contented till my sun sinks in the west;
I will take what fortune sends me and the little I may win,
And be happy on those evenings when a few good friends drop in.

THE BOOK OF MEMORY

Turn me loose and let me be
Young once more and fancy free;
Let me wander where I will,
Down the lane and up the hill,
Trudging barefoot in the dust
In an age that knows no "must,"
And no voice insistently
Speaks of duty unto me;
Let me tread the happy ways
Of those by-gone yesterdays.

Fame had never whispered then,
Making slaves of eager men;
Greed had never called me down
To the gray walls of the town,
Offering frankincense and myrrh
If I'd be its prisoner;
I was free to come and go
Where the cherry blossoms blow,
Free to wander where I would,
Finding life supremely good.

But I turned, as all must do,
From the happiness I knew
To the land of care and strife,

Seeking for a fuller life;
Heard the lure of fame and sought
That renown so dearly bought;
Listened to the voice of greed
Saying: "These the things you need,"
Now the gray town holds me fast,
Prisoner to the very last.

Age has stamped me as its own;
Youth to younger hearts has flown;
Still the cherry blossoms blow
In the land loused to know;
Still the fragrant clover spills
Perfume over dales and hills,
But I'm not allowed to stray
Where the young are free to play;
All the years will grant to me
Is the book of memory.

PRETENDING NOT TO SEE

Sometimes at the table, when
He gets misbehavin', then
Mother calls across to me:
"Look at him, now! Don't you see
What he's doin', sprawlin.' there!
Make him sit up in his chair.
Don't you see the messy way
That he's eating?" An' I say:
"No. He seems all right just now.
What's he doing anyhow?"

Mother placed him there by me,
An' she thinks I ought to see
Every time he breaks the laws
An' correct him, just because
There will come a time some day
When he mustn't act that way.
But I can't be all along
Scoldin' him for doin' wrong.
So if something goes astray,
I jus' look the other way.

Mother tells me now an' then
I'm the easiest o' men,
An' in dealin' with the lad

I will never see the bad
That he does, an' I suppose
Mother's right for Mother knows;
But I'd hate to feel that I'm
Here to scold him all the time.
Little faults might spoil the day,
So I look the other way.

Look the other way an' try
Not to let him catch my eye,
Knowin' all the time that he
Doesn't mean so bad to be;
Knowin', too, that now an' then
I am not the best o' men;
Hopin', too, the times I fall
That the Father of us all,
Lovin', watchin' over me,
Will pretend He doesn't see.

THE JOYS OF HOME

Curling smoke from a chimney low,
And only a few more steps to go,
Faces pressed at a window pane
Watching for someone to come again,
And I am the someone they wait to see—
These are the joys life gives to me.

What has my neighbor excelling this:
A good wife's love and a baby's kiss?
What if his chimneys tower higher?
Peace is found at our humble fire.
What if his silver and gold are more?
Rest is ours when the day is o'er.

Strive for fortune and slave for fame,
You find that joy always stays the same:
Rich man and poor man dream and pray
For a home where laughter shall ever stay,
And the wheels go round and men spend their might
For the few glad hours they may claim at night.

Home, where the kettle shall gaily sing,
Is all that matters with serf or king;
Gold and silver and laurelled fame

Are only sweet when the hearth's aflame
With a cheerful fire, and the loved ones there
Are unafraid of the wolves of care.

So let me come home at night to rest
With those who know I have done my best;
Let the wife rejoice and my children smile,
And I'll know by their love that I am worthwhile,
For this is conquest and world success—
A home where abideth happiness.

WE'RE DREAMERS ALL

Oh, man must dream of gladness wherever his pathways lead,
And a hint of something better is written in every creed;
And nobody wakes at morning but hopes ere the day is o'er
To have come to a richer pleasure than ever he's known before.

For man is a dreamer ever. He glimpses the hills afar
And plans for the joys off yonder where all his tomorrows are;
When trials and cares beset him, in the distance he still can see
A hint of a future splendid and the glory that is to be.

There's never a man among us but cherishes dreams of rest;
We toil for that something better than that which is now our best.
Oh, what if the cup be bitter and what if we're racked with pain?
There are wonderful days to follow when never we'll grieve again.

Back of the sound of the hammer, and back of the hissing steam,
And back of the hand at the throttle is ever a lofty dream;
All of us, great or humble, look over the present need
To the dawn of the glad tomorrow which is promised in every creed.

WHAT IS SUCCESS?

Success is being friendly when another needs a friend;
It's in the cheery words you speak, and in the coins you lend;
Success is not alone in skill and deeds of daring great;
It's in the roses that you plant beside your garden gate.

Success is in the way you walk the paths of life each day;
It's in the little things you do and in the things you say;
Success is in the glad hello you give your fellow man;
It's in the laughter of your home and all the joys you plan.

Success is not in getting rich or rising high to fame;
It's not alone in winning goals which all men hope to claim;
It's in the man you are each day, through happiness or care;
It's in the cheery words you speak and in the smile you wear.

Success is being big of heart and clean and broad of mind;
It's being faithful to your friends, and to the stranger, kind;
It's in the children whom you love, and all they learn from you—
Success depends on character and everything you do.

THE THREE ME'S

I'd like to steal a day and be
All alone with little me,
Little me that used to run
Everywhere in search of fun;
Little me of long ago
Who was glad and didn't know
Life is freighted down with care
For the backs of men to bear;
Little me who thought a smile
Ought to linger all the while—
On his Mother's pretty face
And a tear should never trace
Lines of sorrow, hurt or care
On those cheeks so wondrous fair.

I should like once more to be
All alone with youthful me;
Youthful me who saw the hills
Where the sun its splendor spills
And was certain that in time
To the topmost height he'd climb;
Youthful me, serene of soul,
Who beheld a shining goal.
And imagined he could gain
Glory without grief or pain,

Confident and quick with life,
Madly eager for the strife,
Knowing not that bitter care
Waited for his coming there.

I should like to sit alone
With the me now older grown,
Like to lead the little me
And the youth that used to be
Once again along the ways
Of our glorious yesterdays.
We could chuckle soft and low
At the things we didn't know,
And could laugh to think how bold
We had been in days of old,
And how blind we were to care
With its heartache and despair,
We could smile away the tears
And the pain of later years.

BROTHERS ALL

Under the toiler's grimy shirt,
Under the sweat and the grease and dirt,
Under the rough outside you view,
Is a man who thinks and feels as you.

Go talk with him,
Go walk with him,
Sit down with him by a running stream,
Away from the things that are hissing steam,
Away from his bench,
His hammer and wrench,
And the grind of need
And the sordid deed,
And this you'll find
As he bares his mind:
In the things which count when this life is through
He's as tender and big and as good as you.

Be fair with him,
And share with him
An hour of time in a restful place,
Brother to brother and face to face,
And he'll whisper low
Of the long ago,
Of a loved one dead

And the tears he shed;
And you'll come to see
That in suffering he,
With you, is hurt by the self-same rod
And turns for help to the self-same God.

You hope as he,
You dream of splendors, and so does he;
His children must be as you'd have yours be;
He shares your love
For the Flag above,
He laughs and sings
For the self-same things;
When he's understood
He is mostly good,
Thoughtful of others and kind and true,
Brave, devoted—and much like you.

Under the toiler's grimy shirt,
Under the sweat and the grease and dirt,
Under the rough outside you view,
Is a man who thinks and feels as you.

WHEN WE UNDERSTAND THE PLAN

I reckon when the world we leave
And cease to smile and cease to grieve,
When each of us shall quit the strife
And drop the working tools of life,
Somewhere, somehow, we'll come to find
Just what our Maker had in mind.

Perhaps through clearer eyes than these
We'll read life's hidden mysteries,
And learn the reason for our tears—
Why sometimes came unhappy years,
And why our dearest joys were brief
And bound so closely unto grief.

There is so much beyond our scope,
As blindly on through life we grope,
So much we cannot understand,
However wisely we have planned,
That all who walk this earth about
Are constantly beset by doubt.

No one of us can truly say
Why loved ones must be called away,
Why hearts are hurt, or e'en explain

Why some must suffer years of pain;
Yet some day all of us shall know
The reason why these things are so.

I reckon in the years to come,
When these poor lips of clay are dumb,
And these poor hands have ceased to toil,
Somewhere upon a fairer soil
God shall to all of us make clear
The purpose of our trials here.

THE SPOILER

With a twinkle in his eye
He'd come gayly walkin' by
An' he'd whistle to the children
    An' he'd beckon 'em to come,
Then he'd chuckle low an' say,
"Come along, I'm on my way,
An' it's I that need your company
    To buy a little gum."

When his merry call they'd hear,
All the children, far an' near,
Would come flyin' from the gardens
    Like the chickens after wheat;
When we'd shake our heads an' say:
"No, you mustn't go today!"
He'd beg to let him have 'em
    In a pack about his feet.

Oh, he spoiled 'em, one an' all;
There was not a youngster small
But was over-fed on candy
    An' was stuffed with lollypops,
An' I think his greatest joy
Was to get some girl or boy
An' bring 'em to their parents
    All besmeared by chocolate drops.

Now the children's hearts are sore
For he comes to them no more,
And no more to them he whistles
    And no more for them he stops;
But in Paradise, I think,
With his chuckle and his wink,
He is leading little angels
    To the heavenly candy shops.

A VANISHED JOY

When I was but a little lad of six and seven and eight,
One joy I knew that has been lost in customs up-to-date,
Then Saturday was baking day and Mother used to make,
The while I stood about and watched, the Sunday pies and cake;
And I was there to have fulfilled a small boy's fondest wish,
The glorious privilege of youth—to scrape the frosting dish!

On Saturdays I never left to wander far away—
I hovered near the kitchen door on Mother's baking day;
The fragrant smell of cooking seemed to hold me in its grip,
And naught cared I for other sports while there were sweets to sip;
I little cared that all my chums had sought the brook to fish;
I chose to wait that moment glad when I could scrape the dish.

Full many a slice of apple I have lifted from a pie
Before the upper crust went on, escaping Mother's eye;
Full many a time my fingers small in artfulness have strayed
Into some sweet temptation rare which Mother's hands had made;
But eager-eyed and watery-mouthed, I craved the greater boon,
When Mother let me clean the dish and lick the frosting spoon.

The baking days of old are gone, our children cannot know
The glorious joys that childhood owned and loved so long ago.
New customs change the lives of all and in their heartless way
They've robbed us of the glad event once known as baking day.
The stores provide our every need, yet many a time I wish
Our kids could know that bygone thrill and scrape the frosting dish.

"CARRY ON"

They spoke it bravely, grimly, in their darkest hours of doubt;
They spoke it when their hope was low and when their strength gave
    out;
We heard it from the dying in those troubled days now gone,
And they breathed it as their slogan for the living: "Carry on!"

Now the days of strife are over, and the skies are fair again,
But those two brave words of courage on our lips should still remain;
In the trials which beset us and the cares we look upon,
To our dead we should be faithful—we have still to "carry on!"

"Carry on!" through storm and danger, "carry on" through dark despair,
"Carry on" through hurt and failure, "carry on" through grief and care;
'Twas the slogan they bequeathed us as they fell beside the way,
And for them and for our children, let us "carry on!" today.

LIFE'S SINGLE STANDARD

There are a thousand ways to cheat and a thousand ways to sin;
There are ways uncounted to lose the game, but there's only one way to
    win;
And whether you live by the sweat of your brow or in luxury's garb
    you're dressed,
You shall stand at last, when your race is run, to be judged by the single
    test.

Some men lie by the things they make; some lie in the deeds they do;
And some play false for a woman's love, and some for a cheer or two;
Some rise to fame by the force of skill, grow great by the might of power,
Then wreck the temple they toiled to build, in a single, shameful hour.

The follies outnumber the virtues good; sin lures in a thousand ways;
But slow is the growth of man's character and patience must mark his
    days;
For only those victories shall count, when the work of life is done,
Which bear the stamp of an honest man, and by courage and faith were
    won.

There are a thousand ways to fail, but only one way to win!
Sham cannot cover the wrong you do nor wash out a single sin,
And never shall victory come to you, whatever of skill you do,
Save you've done your best in the work of life and unto your best were
    true.

LEARN TO SMILE

The good Lord understood us when He taught us how to smile;
He knew we couldn't stand it to be solemn all the while;
He knew He'd have to shape us so that when our hearts were gay,
We could let our neighbors know it in a quick and easy way.

So He touched the lips of Adam and He touched the lips of Eve,
And He said: "Let these be solemn when your sorrows make you
    grieve,
But when all is well in Eden and your life seems worth the while,
Let your faces wear the glory and the sunshine of a smile.

"Teach the symbol to your children, pass it down through all the years.
Though they know their share of sadness and shall weep their share of
    tears,
Through the ages men and women shall prove their faith in Me
By the smile upon their faces when their hearts are trouble-free."

The good Lord understood us when He sent us down to earth,
He knew our need for laughter and for happy signs of mirth;
He knew we couldn't stand it to be solemn all the while,
But must share our joy with others—so He taught us how to smile.

THE TRUE MAN

This is the sort of a man was he:
True when it hurt him a lot to be;
Tight in a corner an' knowin' a lie
Would have helped him out, but he wouldn't buy
His freedom there in so cheap a way—
He told the truth though he had to pay.

Honest! Not in the easy sense,
When he needn't worry about expense—
We'll all play square when it doesn't count
And the sum at stake's not a large amount—
But he was square when the times were bad,
An' keepin' his word took all he had.

Honor is something we all profess,
But most of us cheat—some more, some less—
An' the real test isn't the way we do
When there isn't a pinch in either shoe;
It's whether we're true to our best or not
When the right thing's certain to hurt a lot.

That is the sort of a man was he:
Straight when it hurt him a lot to be;
Times when a lie would have paid him well,
No matter the cost, the truth he'd tell;
An' he'd rather go down to a drab defeat
Than save himself if he had to cheat.

CLEANING THE FURNACE

Last night Pa said to Ma: "My dear, it's gettin' on to fall,
It's time I did a little job I do not like at all.
I wisht 'at I was rich enough to hire a man to do
The dirty work around this house an' clean up when he's through,
But since I'm not, I'm truly glad that I am strong an' stout,
An' ain't ashamed to go myself an' clean the furnace out."

Then after supper Pa put on his overalls an' said
He'd work down in the cellar till 'twas time to go to bed.
He started in to rattle an' to bang an' poke an' stir,
An' the dust began a-climbin' up through every register
Till Ma said: "Goodness gracious; go an' shut those things up tight
Or we'll all be suffocated an' the house will be a sight."

Then he carted out the ashes in a basket an' a pail,
An' from cellar door to alley he just left an ashy trail.
Then he pulled apart the chimney, an' 'twas full of something black,
An' he skinned most all his knuckles when he tried to put it back.
We could hear him talkin' awful, an' Ma looked at us an' said:
"I think it would be better if you children went to bed."

When he came up from the cellar there were ashes in his hair,
There were ashes in his eyebrows—but he didn't seem to care—
There were ashes in his mustache, there were ashes in his eyes,
An' we never would have known him if he'd took us by surprise.
"Well, I got it clean," he sputtered, and Ma said: "I guess that's true;
Once the dirt was in the furnace, but now most of it's on you."

TROUBLE BRINGS FRIENDS

It's seldom trouble comes alone. I've noticed this: When things go
    wrong
An' trouble comes a-visitin', it always brings a friend along;
Sometimes it's one you've known before, and then perhaps it's someone
    new
Who stretches out a helping hand an' stops to see what he can do.

If never trials came to us, if grief an' sorrow passed us by,
If every day the sun came out an' clouds were never in the sky,
We'd still have neighbors, I suppose, each one pursuin' selfish ends,
But only neighbors they would be—we'd never know them as our
    friends.

Out of the troubles I have had have come my richest friendships here,
Kind hands have helped to bear my care, kind words have fallen on my
    ear;
An' so I say when trouble comes I know before the storm shall end
That I shall find my bit of care has also brought to me a friend.